Bring Your Teen Back From The Brink

Get Educated, Get Tough, and Get Help to Save Your Teen from Drugs

---

Will Wooton, LAADC, CADC

and

R. Bruce Rowe

Bring Your Teen Back From The Brink:
Get educated, get tough, and get help to save your teen from drugs
Copyright © 2012 by Will Wooton and R. Bruce Rowe

ISBN 978-1477536438

This book is not intended to take the place of advice from a professional drug counselor, but instead is intended to be an educational guide for parents. Readers are advised to consult a drug counselor, medical doctor, psychologist, or other trained professional for the treatment of alcoholism or drug addiction. Neither the publisher nor authors take any responsibility for any possible consequences from any of the recommendations or resources contained in this book.

Table of Contents

Chapter 8 – The Elements of an Effective Program 103

Chapter 9 – Stories From Parents Like You 115

Chapter 10 – Stories From Those in Recovery 157

Appendices 189

Introduction

My kid is on drugs, what do I do? That's the question this book will answer.

The treatment of substance abuse is becoming a reality for more families every year. According to a national study released in June 2011 by The National Center of Addiction and Substance Abuse (CASA) (Adolescent Substance Use: America's #1 Public Health Problem), 9 out of 10 Americans who meet the medical criteria for addiction started smoking, drinking, or using other drugs before age 18.

Though several drugs show declining use among adolescents over the past five years (National Institute on Drug Abuse "Monitoring the Future" survey), the 2011 survey turned up a few "areas of concern":

- Daily Marijuana use increased again among 8th, 10th, and 12th graders from 2010 to 2011. Among 12th graders it was at its highest point since the early 1980s.
- Though many claim that marijuana is harmless and non-addicting, the daily use figures reported in the survey show a definite upward annual trend as teens continue to use. Prevalence levels of daily use in 2011 are 1.3% for 8th graders, 3.6% for 10th grade teens, and 6.6% for seniors.
- Marijuana use among teens rose in 2011 for the fourth straight year—a sharp contrast to the considerable decline that had occurred in the preceding decade. Daily marijuana use is now at a 30-year peak level among high school seniors.
- Past-year use of marijuana was reported by 14 percent of 8th-graders, 28 percent of 10th-graders, and 35 percent of seniors.
- After marijuana, prescription and over-the-counter medications account for most of the top drugs abused by seniors in the past year.
- While use of Ecstasy held steady during the past year, use in all three grades is above the recent low points by 33%, 85%, and 77%, respectively, suggesting that a rebound seen in recent years

is primarily among older teens.

- In what may be a switch to drugs, alcohol use - and occasions of heavy drinking (five or more drinks on the same occasion) - continued a long-term gradual decline among teens, reaching historically low levels in 2011. Over the past 20 years, from 1991 to 2011, the proportion of 8th graders reporting any use of alcohol in the prior 30 days has fallen by about half (from 25% to 13%), among 10th graders by more than one third (from 43% to 27%), and among seniors by about one fourth (from 54% to 40%).

In March 2010 the nation's emergency physicians issued a warning to parents about the increasing use of prescription drugs among teens, which is now the second leading class of abused drugs, after marijuana. The results of a recent survey by American College of Emergency Physicians (ACEP) showed that nearly three-quarters of a million people needed emergency care because of prescription drug abuse.

Though overall use is declining, alcohol still tops the list of intoxicating substances used by underage youth – who are also more likely to engage in dangerous binge drinking – than any other illicit drug or tobacco in the U.S., according to the U.S. Department of Health and Human Services. Other facts about alcohol use by young people from the 2010 National Survey on Drug Use and Health:

- The rate of current alcohol use among youths aged 12 to 17 was 13.6%, but 40% of high school seniors reported the use of alcohol in the prior 30 days.
- There were an estimated ten million underage drinkers in 2010, including 6.5 million binge drinkers and two million heavy drinkers.
- Fifty five percent of current drinkers aged 12 to 20 reported that their last use of alcohol in the past month occurred in someone else's home, and 29.9% reported that it had occurred in their own home.
- Among the 12 to 20 age group who did not pay for the alcohol they last drank, more than one in five (nearly 22%) got it from **a**

parent, guardian, or other adult family member.

- Adults aged 21 or older who had first used alcohol at age 14 or younger were more than five times as likely to be classified with alcohol dependence or abuse than adults who had their first drink at age 21 or older (15.1% vs. 2.7%).

Finally, new threats are constantly researched, manufactured, and promoted, not just by drug dealers, but by legitimate food and beverage companies.

One of the latest to appear was Caffeinated Alcoholic Beverages or CABs. The drinks experienced rapid growth in popularity, with two leading brands together forging a 67-fold increase in sales, from 337,500 gallons in 2002 (the first year of significant CAB production) to a reported *22 million gallons* in 2008.

Fortunately the FDA banned the sale of CABs in December 2010, but the sweet drinks continue to be sold as alcoholic beverages. One popular brand features a 23.5 ounce can with an alcohol content that is the equivalent of four to five beers. The makers pack the easy-to-drink beverages with 6-12% alcohol content, depending on what each state allows.

We will also tell you about the latest round of what is being pushed to your teens as "safe" alternatives to illegal drugs, with innocent sounding names, like spice and bath salts. The drive for the next high is constantly spawning new formulations.

Experience backs up the numbers

All those numbers are very important, and dangerous, statistics that mirror what I see daily as a professional drug counselor to teens. The pages ahead will explain why.

The reason for this book is to help answer some of the questions that we professionals hear on a regular basis. The commonalities that we see among families facing this situation have made treatment, at times, a series of standard mental checklists that counselors sort through and adapt to effect change in teen attitudes and drug abuse. We want to show you that you are not alone. Many, many parents just like you have been down this road before.

This book, by design, will help guide your family through your own war on drugs. As a counselor who has worked with teens for more than ten years, I do call it a war. It's a dirty, painful, draining, stressful battle at times, and it must be looked at as such. Very often you'll gain only small victories, and you will suffer setbacks as well, but every step will lead you to the ultimate goal: pulling your teen back from the brink of self-destruction.

Not our child

The number one question I have been asked again and again is, "How did we not see this happening in our home?" The answer is simple. Kids have made drug abuse a fine art, at times making it their focus to behave outrageously, yet all the while inducing you to think that you are crazy for suspecting something is wrong. The goal of teenagers is to push the limits you set and get away with it.

Parental denial of the problem is a very powerful tool that kids use to their advantage. Denial is the number one focus of many of the groups that I facilitate. Denial in the form of "my kids are not like those kids", and also that this is the type of problem that will just go away when you tell them to stop. As anyone who has had a teenager will tell you, it can be a daily challenge to deal with normal teenage behavior, but adding drugs into the mix makes a toxic combination that compounds the turmoil. Left unaddressed, it will leave your family in crisis for years to come.

More than just getting clean

With teens, drug abuse in itself is rarely the only problem. The ultimate problem is actually the behavior and the decisions that they make while under the influence. Anger, negative attitude towards the family, poor motivation to achieve or even set goals, failing academic performance, and depression are the hallmark signs that someone is abusing drugs.

As parents you may feel that these behaviors are a passing phase for your child. You remember similar things that the teenage-you or your friends may have been through. You'll say, "I made it through, so what's the big deal if my kid is experimenting too?" You may go so far as to try to parent as if you can reason with your teen, while hoping that if you relate to them, then they'll be safe.

Hope on your part is a wonderful thing, but not without solid action. Your teen's friends should be made at social settings or school, not at home. Your child is not your friend and treating them like a new buddy to do things with is just poor parenting.

But your child is the most precious gift that you have. Along with that gift comes tremendous responsibility. Step up to the plate and tackle that responsibility head on through discipline, reinforcement, role modeling, and love.

I have seen many families that could not handle me telling them what they needed to change in order for their child to change; some walk out of group in the middle of a session. They may say that they just want their child to "cut down" on drinking alcohol or marijuana, and focus more on school. If that's where you are, then I highly encourage you to read this book as fast as you can.

Educate yourself as your teens do

With the advancement of technology – the Internet, instant messaging, social networking, cell phones, hundreds of TV channels – kids have access to more information (most of it incorrect) about drugs and the short- and long-term effects. If your kids are educating each other, you must do the same.

But there hasn't been an efficient way for parents to get that information quickly. *Bring Your Teen Back From The Brink* is designed to do that.

In this book, we will tell you what you can expect your teen to say and do. We'll also teach you about popular street terms for each drug and how each is ingested. From simple household objects used to get high, through advanced paraphernalia bought through the Internet, kids are becoming more resourceful not only with what they take, but how to get it. And of course, we will bring you information on what you can do to save your child from this destructive behavior.

The changes that you will need to make might be hard and most likely will feel unnatural, but they are essential to changing your child's behavior.

Tear it down to build it up

Have you seen a total house remodel? It starts with a demolition that is a dirty, dusty, chaotic mess. Only one wall or room might be left standing. When you first see that stripped structure, you probably can't imagine the beautiful new home that will be built in its place. But with lots of patience and time – and of course a dollar investment too – you'll get something that looks and feels like the vision you've had in your mind all along.

That could easily describe bringing your child back from drug and alcohol abuse as well.

I invite all parents to sit down and write out a description of the kind of person you want your child to become as they grow and mature: healthy, responsible, honest, trustworthy, motivated, etc. (See the chart at the end of this introduction.) Now look at the reality of what your child's beliefs and actions are right now. Do they match up? If not, don't feel like you have failed as a parent. You haven't. But now is the time to educate yourself and take action.

Leading your teen through this process and back to a healthy, productive life is possible. I have seen hundreds of families move from total dysfunction to becoming a supportive group of individuals who grow together and share strength to help achieve recovery. Through this book I hope I can play a part in that process.

Exercise 1 – Reality Check

Reality Check		
When your child was born, what did you want for them? How did you see their lives unfolding? What milestones and achievements did you expect of them? What moments did you want to enjoy with them? Answer in terms of the different facets of their life below.		
	Expectation	**Reality**
Family (Spend time together? Happy, loving, cooperative, grateful…? Mindful or defiant? Contributing or taking? Conforming to your beliefs or faith)		
School (Grades and attendance? Does effort and achievement match potential? Will they graduate high school, college? Just getting by or taking full advantage?)		
Personal (Integrity and honesty? Thinking of others or egocentric? Treating others with respect? Humble or arrogant? Gravitating to positive or negative influences, e.g., music, TV, etc.? Physical appearance?)		
Friends (Positive or negative? Achievers? Respectful, supportive, open, accepting? Appearance?)		
Activities/Sports (Finding something to be passionate about? Gaining or losing desire? Achieving to their potential? Working to be better? Having fun? Coachable?)		

Chapter One - Playing A Game That's Been Played

The title of this chapter was inspired by the words of a teen in recovery, as he spoke to another teen who was still trying to play the game of lying, manipulation, and denial regarding their own drug abuse. Certainly each individual is different, with different circumstances and turns in the plot, but the story of teen drug abuse is amazingly predictable. It's a story that repeats over and over as kids experiment with drugs.

For the following story, we've created a character named Jacob, a fictitious name, but whose story contains real elements from real stories. Though the following is written from a male point of view, it can apply to your female child as well.

Jacob's story

Jacob is a junior in high school. He's always earned good grades – mostly As and Bs. Lately, though, his motivation has suffered. His behavior at school has become a concern over the past couple of years, and teacher conferences are on the rise.

When progress reports come out, he is missing assignments. At home, the nightly battle over homework is escalating. He feels like he doesn't need to do it. As he argues, and as the record shows, he's earned good grades in the past. He wants you to stop micromanaging him.

Soon, the attendance office is calling to tell you that he's missing classes, or even entire days of school.

Don't you know? Things have changed.

Over the past few years, he has grown more and more disrespectful with you, and with any authority figure. Teachers, coaches, and especially you, are the target of his increasingly arrogant, know-it-all attitude. His language, manners, and actions are totally inappropriate for anywhere but a locker room, yet here they are, right in your face.

"It's no big deal," he tells you. Times are different now, and he says any behavior he sees or language he hears on TV should be OK for the home as well. Of course, most of the TV he's watching these days is a constant flow of disrespectful behavior, challenging authority, everything-is-fair-game humor, and approval – even expectation – of drug use.

Once an athlete, Jacob's primary goals now are to sleep in late, play video games, avoid any activity that requires real effort of any kind, and hang out with friends for as many hours of the day as possible.

What's your problem?

You, of course, are the "psycho parent." No other parents care about such a downward spiral of bad behavior in their kids. No others ask where their child is going at night, who they're hanging out with, or set a curfew any earlier than midnight. No other parents are asking their child to get to school on time, do their homework, or come home right after school. Apparently you are the only ones in your community who have these expectations.

He dares you to deal with him. More and more he actively disobeys and ignores what you tell him. He willingly tells you he doesn't care about any consequences you might impose. To Jacob, it's "worth it" to continue doing exactly what he wants to do.

Then it happens. He comes home very late, or maybe you catch him sneaking back into the house late at night, when you thought he was already home in bed. Or he might show up at school obviously intoxicated. Jacob may or may not smell of pot smoke or alcohol; kids are good at masking any odors. But his red eyes and sluggish or wobbly appearance belie the signs of drug or alcohol use.

That's when Jacob begins to do what he does best – lie.

It was just a few times

Jacob says he was just out with some friends and they had drugs or alcohol in the house or car or park, or wherever they were hanging out. They pushed him to try it. He did it this one time, he says. He may admit to using three or four times ever in his life. He's absolutely not a regular user. Then he reminds you, "You did this kind of stuff when you were my age."

And of course, "It's no big deal."

You react with a grounding for the next week or weekend. He may or may not comply. But the behavior does not stop.

That gut feeling you have that something's just not right is growing. Many times, you'll begin to hear rumors, or direct reports, of your child's behavior and involvement with drugs from other parents, school administrators, or even other kids.

It'll be OK, I can take care of him

Yet, this is your child. The parent in you wants to trust him. That's ingrained in you as a parent. Every kid goes through this right? You think, we "all" go through some experimentation and pushing of the boundaries at this age. You probably really believe that this is just a phase that will resolve itself. Or maybe you just hope so because you don't want to deal with it.

Jacob knows how much you love him, and how much you want to believe what he says. That you think you can take care of the problem yourself. Sadly, he knows he can use that against you. This is where the manipulation, lying, denial, and rationalization begin to accelerate.

You catch him again. This time you find drug paraphernalia in his clothing, backpack or room. It's undeniable what Jacob is doing, but he won't admit anything.

Jacob's story:

- The marijuana pipe is not his, but belongs to a friend
- He's only experimented with it over the past month or so
- Someone hid the stuff in his car without him knowing it
- The last time he smoked was a week or two ago
- It's "only" pot, he hates alcohol, and he thinks other drugs are dangerous and stupid
- He's researched marijuana on the Internet, and there are lots of well-educated people who think there is nothing wrong with it
- Pot has health benefits, and it's going to be legal soon anyway

17

- It's a plant, not a drug
- Lots of famous, successful people use pot with no problem
- It's in the bible and Jesus smoked it
- He can stop any time he wants to
- It's no big deal
- He tried to call you to let you know where he was, but his cell phone wouldn't work
- You're the only parent who cares this much, and you're a psycho for being so over-protective
- And he's "almost" an adult now and can make his own choices
- He's telling you the truth, and you need to stop being so mean and trust him
- Your lack of trust is hurting your relationship and driving him away from the family

The real story:
- The pipe does belong to him – and it's not the first one he's owned
- The first time he tried marijuana was in middle school, most likely at 13 or 14 years old
- He's smoking and using every chance he can get, and probably has done so for several months now
- Marijuana in itself is a powerful drug, with long-term detrimental effects, but Jacob most likely has begun to experiment with other drugs as well
- You can find "facts" to back up any argument on the Internet
- Even if it were legal, he would be too young to use it
- He drinks easily-obtainable beer, in the popular 40-ounce variety that somehow has become the standard these days
- It is most certainly a big deal, and without the right plan to help him, he is headed down a predictable path to harder stuff, more of it, and big problems in his life
- While a growing problem, it's still only a minority of high school kids who smoke it

- Funny how *you* never have so many cell phone problems
- Is it over-protective to be worried about who he's associating with as he obtains and uses drugs, or where he is and what he's doing while under the influence?
- His immature brain has a long way to go before he'll make rational choices – not to mention he's living in *your* house, is reliant on *you* for everything he has, and he needs to obey *your* rules
- While he's using drugs, he's lying most of the time and you need to question everything he says

Jacob is in full defense mode now. His goal is to throw you off track in any way possible so he can get you off his back and continue doing what he wants to do.

Sound familiar? We've got a plan for you.

Your job is to get educated on this whole new world of teen drug abuse so you can stop, or at least disrupt, the predictable downward spiral and bring your child back to reality.

That reality doesn't necessarily mean that they need to go to college, get a job, get married, etc. That is a scary and often unappealing prospect for a teenager (and for many of us adults as a matter of fact). Remember that even off drugs, they're still teens, and most likely they aren't going to listen to "old people" like you anyway.

What it does mean is that they begin facing life as it comes, with a clear head and without medication, keeping as many doors open for themselves as possible. The path of drug use is a very narrow one, with limited options at best and jail or death at the worst.

You need to learn as much as you can, as quickly as possible, and that's what the chapters ahead are designed to deliver. We'll show you many aspects of what you are going through, or will soon encounter, as you live out your version of the story you've just read. Here's some of what you'll learn:

- What your teen will say and do
- How you'll feel

- The language of drug abuse, descriptions of common drugs, and what to look for to know what your teen is doing
- How the mind of the user works
- How to deal with suspected drug use, and the elements of an effective program
- Stories from parents like you and teens in recovery, who tell you what worked for them, what didn't, and how to find a happy ending

Chapter 2 - What Your Teen Will Say

Once your teenage child thinks you might be aware of their drug use, they will resort to a number of tactics to throw you off the track, so they can continue their behavior. The following paragraphs describe some of those tactics.

One good story (lie) deserves another

This is often the most difficult behavior for parents to understand. In most cases you have devoted your life to providing for your child, and to paving a smooth path for their life. You literally took care of their every need for many years. Later you filled their days with fun things to do. And always, you loved them. You think they'll be grateful for that and treat you with respect and gratitude.

Not so.

Some children begin to lie at an early age, but most are the sweet, innocent child that you imagined, until they become adolescents. Deep inside, they probably do still love you, but teenagers - especially those with something to hide - become centered on themselves and resort to a number of familiar lies to get what they want. Here's just a sample of what you'll hear:

- I only did it that one time
- It isn't mine, it belongs to my friend
- I only smoke pot
- I haven't smoked in a week
- It's only cigarette smoke, you don't even know what pot smells like
- I *was* with them, but I wasn't doing anything, only they were
- Alcohol (or pills, or cocaine, or whatever drug you suspect) is stupid and I would never do that
- I was at (insert parent-approved friend name's) house all night
- We went to the movies (ask for details of the plot and see what they say)

- I've done the research and pot is perfectly safe
- It's just a lifestyle choice, and I can handle it
- I'm not stupid enough to get hooked
- I think I might be depressed/have anxiety/(insert psychiatric diagnosis here)
- You did it.

When your child's lies multiply, most likely you'll get an unsettled feeling in your gut when they talk to you. Pay attention to that feeling. Not the one that says, "He's right. Everything will probably be okay," but the one that tells you, "Something is just not right."

He's one of my *good* friends

They know you love them and want to trust them. They know you feel guilty when you think you may be doing something to hurt their feelings, break a promise, or be that "unfair" parent. They also know that you think you can make everything better with a hug, and by just piling on more love. After all, that's what you've done since they were infants.

Surprisingly, despite the fact that they owe everything they have to you – and that you have invested years into their growth and well-being – they will use that information to manipulate you as much as possible. Here's a sample dialog that may sound familiar to you:

"You need to stop what you're doing. Look at what's going on with you."

"Dad, it's not that big of a deal."

"Look at all these zeroes you're getting at school."

"It's just busy work and I don't need to do it to get decent grades. I'm almost 15 and I can make my own decisions. Besides, my teacher hates me. She's always picking on me in class. Everyone does things, but I'm the one who gets in trouble."

"Like what? What does she do?"

(Already they've got you off track. This has nothing to do with the teacher/coach/counselor/lunch-area monitor, yet here you go "discussing" it with him or her.)

"The other day we were just sitting at lunch…"(The details of these pointless conversations are irrelevant. You've been had.)

Yet, in a moment of clarity you try to get back to your point.

"You know all this doesn't matter, you need to quit smoking pot and hanging out with those friends of yours. You're grounded for the weekend."

"Dad, you already promised I could go to Jenny's birthday on Saturday. At least let me do that. Besides, you guys know Jenny doesn't screw around, and her parents are always there to make sure we don't do anything."

"OK, Saturday night is fine, but Friday and Sunday, you need to be home."

You don't want to break a "promise", right? You don't want to be too strict…like your parents were. Or maybe you feel guilty as a single parent. So now you're negotiating and they've got their freedom on Saturday night.

She's out of the house and that's all she needs. When will she leave for the birthday party? You can be sure she'll negotiate that with you. When will she come home? You set a curfew and she breaks it. So what? She already has to stay home on Sunday, and there's plenty of time to work on you to get her way for next weekend.

And do you think she'll just stay at Jenny's the whole night? Jenny's parents think she's a great kid. Your child makes sure of that with their best behavior, which of course will open up more wiggle room with those parents. A good story will easily win permission to leave their house, even if it's only for 30 minutes. Plenty of time to hit the bong a few times, then return. Most likely smelling like perfume and breath mints. (See **Chapter 3 - What Your Teen Will Do.**)

As the old saying goes: Give them an inch and they'll take a mile.

While the previous scenario may be a little simplistic, you know the routine. You may not even realize it, but now you've set the pattern. They will now weasel into the cracks of your armor. For a while, it will be an easy game for them to win, but with more knowledge, you'll seal up those cracks, and stop them cold.

But Mom, I've been much better

Hand-in-hand with manipulation, another tactic you'll see from your child is that they will remind you of every good thing they've done recently.

Beware of these things you'll hear:

- I got an A on my history test. (Don't pay attention to those zeros on all the other assignments.)
- I did my chores all week. (Not very well of course, and absolutely nothing more than that.)
- I've been good this week. (Except for when I cussed at you when we argued. Twice.)
- I went to school all week. (One week out of the last eight. Way to go.)
- I love you. (Now it's time to really be suspicious.)
- I'm cutting back. I only smoked pot last week, and only one time. (???)

This is another time when you need to step back and see the big picture. Remind your teen – and yourself – that going to school, doing homework, obeying rules, and being respectful to you are all things that normal kids are expected to do. Brief compliance with any of these behaviors is not cause for celebration, hugs, and restoring revoked privileges and trust. Any child can be on good behavior for a few days or a week. Trust me, you'll feel lousy and be kicking yourself in a few days if you give in to this teenage ploy. Most times they will go right back to doing as they please within a few days.

Yes, acknowledge improvement, but after breaking your trust, your child needs to work for many weeks or months to really make a change that regains your trust and shows you that their good behavior is real.

It's only pot

Run "marijuana is good" through Google and you will find somewhere over ten million results.

The point is, in this Internet age, kids can find millions of sources to back their claim that marijuana is not harmful, and in fact, does all kinds of good things for you. Your teen may tell you that they've "done the research" and that you are sadly misinformed if you think it is harmful. What they are engaged in is not the mindless act of getting high, they'll say, they have made a "lifestyle choice" to enjoy this natural plant that is part of God's green earth.

While there are doctors and scientists who say there are some benefits to weed smoking, your child will be the rare one indeed if they stop smoking at the medicinal dosage. In fact, as their habit builds, you will see that they will find every conceivable way to cram heavier and heavier hits of this drug into their bodies. More about that later.

There is an ongoing scientific study of the increasing potency of pot at the University of Mississippi, called the Potency Monitoring Project. Since 1976, the project has been analyzing samples of marijuana, hash oil, and hashish obtained in seizures by the U.S. Drug Enforcement Administration (DEA). According to their latest report, analyzing data collected from 1,500 seizures in 2008, the average concentration of tetrahydrocannabinol (THC), the active drug in marijuana, was 10.1%. That's more than double the average THC concentration of 4% in samples from 1983. In the 2008 samples, about 40% returned results of 9% THC concentrations or higher. The highest concentration was 27.3%.

But, as told on another website we found, we're sure your teenager will just dial back his or her consumption if the pot is more potent than usual. Yeah right.

There is certainly no room here for a full discussion of the safety or dangers of marijuana. Just observe what happens as your teen indulges in their new "lifestyle choice." If they are like most teens, they will lose motivation, become increasingly dependent on the drug to feel "normal", and soon get involved in the greater drug culture. It's a predictable path to more potent and dangerous drugs.

Medicinal marijuana clinics? Please. When we confronted one pot smoking teen his reply was, "I got my card [expletive deleted]! I can smoke all I want." There are countless doctors in on this scam who will gladly issue a prescription card for the right price. Just ask yourself, "Where are most of these 'clinics'?" Here in San Diego County, you will find them either in neighborhoods where young people go to hang out and drink or in suburbs where pot sellers can reach their teen target market.

Do what your kids are doing on the Internet. Get on the computer, start searching, and learn all you can.

It's no big deal and besides, you did it too

Most likely your teen will try to minimize their own drug habit by reminding you of your wilder days. "You did it, so why shouldn't I have my chance."

First, your past behavior has nothing to do with your child's behavior. They still live in your house, under your rules, and within the confines of the law. When they move out of the house, then they can think about making their own choices.

Maybe you can remember a time when you easily could have ended up with a DUI, caused an accident or injury, or worse, caused someone else's death or your own. Think back to a time when you were completely vulnerable because of your loss of control due to being intoxicated. Do you want your son or daughter to find themselves in that state, just so they can have this highly questionable "rite of passage"?

Instead, make every effort to pass along your experience to your teen. Tell them about those stories of loss of control and danger. If they don't listen and start to change their behavior, you'll know if your child has passed the experimentation stage and moved into more frequent drug use. Normal kids usually don't have to learn that fire burns by sticking their hand in the flame.

Together with the previous stats on the potency of today's weed, suffice it to say that you most likely never smoked anything like your teen is smoking now. And you never had access to the cornucopia of prescription drugs that can be had in any high school in America (yes, any high school).

Remember, you're an adult, and they are still very much the child. Use this and all the other information you'll get from this book to bypass these tired tactics and help your teenager get better.

Also know that some parents smoke weed or dispense alcohol as well. Some will rationalize that if they have their kids do it at home, where they can monitor and control the pot and alcohol so their kids are "safe," then it's good parenting since kids all do it anyway, right?

Remember the previous stat we shared in the Introduction: Adults aged 21 or older who had first used alcohol at age 14 or younger were more than five times as likely to be classified with alcohol dependence or abuse than adults who had their first drink at age 21 or older. So these parents aren't doing their kids any favors, to say the least.

Unfortunately, there's no fool proof way to discover which parents may be covering up endorsement of their kids use…other than the fact that your teen may want to hang out at certain houses *way* more than others. Just be aware of the possibility and, especially once you've caught your teen using, build a parent network to be informed and spread the word.

You make me want to use!

Divorce. Change of schools. Moving. Lessons or activities they don't want to do. All of these are reasons they will bring up to thrust the blame on you. This is a classic move of the teen drug user as they try to get you to back down when you begin to take action.

Yes, you may be stricter than other parents. You may want to move to a new neighborhood, away from old friends. That's your choice. There are many decisions parents need to make as they raise a family. But don't let your child use this as an excuse to blame you for their actions.

Don't buy into this tactic and start walking on egg shells around your teen. Life isn't always smooth and happy. You need to teach your teen to deal with the ups and downs in a healthy way, not turn to medication every time they have a bump in the road.

I'm going to be 18 soon, then I can do whatever I want

Pretty simple answer here: "OK."

This is not meant to be a flip answer, but be sure to change the locks when they leave. If things have reached this stage, you need to protect yourself, your family, and your house from them when they decide to come back. And they almost always *will* come back.

Before they go, just let them know that you love them and will be ready to get them help when they're ready. They'll ignore you now, but will know your support is waiting when they hit bottom and want to get clean.

If they want to try it on their own, then let them give it a shot. Ninety-nine percent of teenagers have very limited street smarts. They'll think they have everything figured out. They may even know a friend or two who will let them hang out at their place and crash on their couch for awhile. But they haven't got a clue about what it *really* takes to live on their own. Especially when they're under the influence and have the constant expense of supporting a habit.

They'll find that life in a garage or crappy apartment is not a happy one. They'll be associating with other drug users 24 hours a day, seven days a week. Those "friends' will lie, cheat, and steal to take advantage of them, just as your teen has done to you.

Girls may think they have it easier by latching onto a boyfriend when they leave home. It's true that they absolutely will have no shortage of guys willing to be with them for a while. But we all know that females actually face additional dangers, in terms of sexual and physical abuse at the hands of a male whose mind is warped by drug abuse.

For you, this is also a turning point. Once your teen is no longer a minor, your responsibilities are greatly reduced, at least from a legal standpoint. Now they are responsible for their own actions. If they won't obey the rules of your house, then you can freely kick them out. You don't have to provide even the bare essentials, as you do when they are still a minor.

If they return and get into your house without your permission, you can call the police. And in the worse cases, when other avenues are exhausted and you need to back them into a corner, you can have them put in jail. That's real jail, not a cushy juvenile hall.

Obviously this is a last resort. Jail will teach your teen more about the dark side of life than they will scare them into sobriety. But sometimes that is a tool you can use to force them into seeing that addiction or alcoholism is ruining their lives.

Finally, while you may think you need to get help and/or treatment for your child before they turn 18, or you'll lose your ability to force them into a program, that is not necessarily true. As described previously, you actually have a few more weapons at your disposal. You'll just need some patience while they burn their bridges and run out of options.

For all teens of this age, lack of sleep, poor health, no money, dealing drugs, and escalating abuse will get the best of them. Most end up on the streets or in jail as the string of couches runs out. Usually within three to six months, the vast majority of drug abusing teens will realize it's a dead end.

Then, very often, they'll be ready to accept the help that you're ready to give them.

Chapter 3 - What Your Teen Will Do

There are a number of behaviors common to teen drug users. Many of them are also normal adolescent behavior, so there is sometimes a fine line in determining what is the usual teen attitude and what isn't. But if your teenager is building a drug habit, the frequency and degree of each behavior will most likely increase.

Chip away at your rules

In one teen counseling group, a parent told the story of how pathetically low her standards had become as her teenage child's bad behavior escalated. In the face of defiance, running away, skipping school, and frequent drug use, she "celebrated" even the most basic good behavior. Behavior that in reality should be expected from any normal teen.

Look again at the chart you filled out at the end of the introduction. It's amazing how low you can let your standards and expectations slip. Parents, faced with a teen who does almost nothing, will lose perspective on the rules of the house:

- TV shows that used to be blocked, now are accepted into the home, no matter how much gross, authority-flaunting, and self-indulgent content they contain
- Homework time that used to be firmly fixed before dinner, and before TV or video game time, now slides into the late hours of the night "as long as he gets it done"
- Sunday nights once reserved for family time now become yet another night for the teen to hang out with friends
- Vacations and family activities either are centered around what the teen wants to do, or don't happen at all, just to keep the peace
- Chores are done sloppily or not at all
- Expectations for school attendance and grades slide further and further down the curve
- Forbidden language and disrespect are now tolerated just to avoid even larger   confrontations

- Curfews extend
- You begin negotiating over which (or how much) drugs or alcohol is acceptable to abuse

If this situation hasn't hit your house yet, congratulations. But beware of this slippery slope that even the best parents often slide down for months and years. If you find yourself with a child who is non-functional in this way, you've got a teen who needs treatment, even in the rare case they aren't using drugs.

Openly defy you

All through their life, you've been able to control your child most of the time. If you said they had to stay home, they did it. When you forbid them from seeing certain friends, they complied. Chores were done regularly. Begrudgingly maybe, but usually they got done.

But most likely you've seen a major shift in behavior. Unlike most kids, your teenager has discovered that you can't really control them. His or her adrenaline may be flowing the first time they look you in the eye and walk out the door against your wishes, but once they discover they can do it, it gets easier and easier. They know that outside of physical force, you can't stop them. That virtually no parent will resort to a physical fight with their child. And they shouldn't, because it tends to worsen the situation rather than establish how "tough" or strict you are.

Your teenager's attitude, in search of getting high with friends, will become warped in a way that you cannot comprehend. Here are a few attitude changes to look for in a budding addict:
- Tired all the time
- Lacks incentive, ambition, and energy to get things done
- Doesn't care about much of anything: indifference
- Personal hygiene deteriorates; fewer showers, dirty clothes
- Loses interest in extracurricular interests like sports and hobbies
- Anxious, on-edge, and sometimes even paranoid
- Abrupt mood shifts; zero-to-angry in 30 seconds
- Profanity and aggression towards you and others in the family
- Lack of respect for   authority figures

- Leaves the house to "take a walk" for short times
- Hours shift to nocturnal: late nights, waking in mid-day
- Avoids school work and/or going to school
- Secretive and protective of friends and activities
- Lying, even when they don't need to
- Stealing – money, credit cards, valuables, prescription drugs
- Lack of tolerance toward others who are different than themselves
- Pulls away from the family and family activities
- Spends virtually all their time at home in their room
- Vigorously defends, even romanticizes, drug use

Sneak out and/or run away

Is your teen sneaking out at night after you are asleep? Don't be too sure that you know the answer to that question. Often this behavior starts surprisingly young, during the middle school years. They'll use the front door, or, if they have to, a window, even in a second story room where they can get onto the roof. From there, they'll climb down a wall or fence to freedom, and a night of adventure with their friends.

Check your teen's room and see how they might get out. If you have a two-story, look for places where your roof is particularly low or is adjacent to a fence or wall that they can climb up and down. If you can, move them from any room where the window opens out to the roof. Footprints or scuff marks on the wall or house are a good indicator that they are out and on their way at night, as are roof tiles that are broken or loose.

Screw the screens shut if you have to. It's a little inconvenient, but they can still push their way out in an emergency. Set your security alarm at night, but don't be surprised if they can defeat that as well. Your teen will be surprisingly resourceful when it comes to getting their way.

Later in the cycle, your teen will likely run away for a day, or two or three. You won't know for sure where they are, but most likely they'll be couch-hopping, sleeping in someone's car, or having a sleep-over where they've convinced the parents that it's all okay with you.

You'll probably get glowing reports on your terrible teen from other families. Part of the game is for your teen to be on their best behavior at other's houses so they can be welcomed there and gain freedom outside your home.

Ignore school work

Your drug-using teen will probably be able to maintain acceptable, even high, grades at first. It will be part of their ammunition in manipulating you and deflecting your attempt to stop their other bad behavior, including drug use.

"His grades are still good," you'll tell yourself. "How bad could it be?"

The answer is that grades really aren't a good barometer of your teen's behavior, especially in the early stages of a developing drug habit. Some kids are able to function at a very high level even while using for several years. In fact, I've seen many teens regularly abusing stimulants who get straight A's.

You know those "good kids" your kid hangs out with? They could easily be getting high with your son or daughter. They're just better at hiding it.

But usually, in the long term, grades will begin to slide as motivation decreases under the effects of drugs. Freshman, sophomore, even junior years of high school may be fine, but typically the second half of high school brings skipping homework, skipping class, truancy, and failing grades in one or more classes.

Obsession with friends and going out

Most of the previous behaviors stem from this one. As soon as they're awake, your teen will be on the phone and Internet finding out who they can hang out with. Then shortly after that, they'll be out the door if you let them (or, as we've discussed, even if you don't).

They will try to stretch the hours they can be gone, and the number of days they can go. Generally it begins with Friday and Saturday nights, but the drug-seeking teen will soon think that's not nearly enough.

They'll begin to bargain for weeknights and Sundays too, and, of course, every day during vacations.

You will begin to dread weekends and holidays because that means it's time for you and your teen to butt heads over this issue, then worry where they are and what they're doing.

Initially your child will likely sleep more, rising in the early afternoon if they can. But with the advance to more highly addictive drugs, your teen will actually begin to sleep less and less, and rise earlier and earlier to leave home, because they need the drug or alcohol more and more to stave off the ill feelings of being without it.

Risky behavior

So what activities fall under the "hanging out" umbrella for your teen? If you can imagine it, they're most likely already doing it:

- Parties – Neighborhood, college frat, beach, park, "cool parents" house
- Party buses that have no destination, but serve as a safe haven for teen alcohol and drug use
- "Kickbacks" – Just another name for parties; see above
- Vandalism
- Physical fights with other kids
- Shoplifting
- Trespassing into schools, empty homes, etc.
- Underage driving
- Casual sex
- Road trips (looong road trips)

You should definitely guard the keys to your car every night. Maybe even keep track of the mileage. Your 14 year-old may be out driving the freeways at night.

You may be surprised one day to find out that when your teen was supposed to be sleeping at a neighborhood friend's house, they were actually a hundred miles or more away from your community at a party or drug-friendly house.

Kids involved in these types of behaviors almost always get caught at some point, resulting in arrest and time in juvenile hall or jail. That often means felony charges, not simple misdemeanor offenses.

As kids get involved in the drug culture, they will begin associating with friends who deal drugs, and may even begin selling drugs as well. Think about it. They have a craving for the substance and it costs money. The haze of drug use takes the stigma away from something that once would seem unthinkable. They are easily lured by putting up "seed money" to finance their dealer friends, with an expected return on their "investment." They know lots of willing customers. It's only a short leap (fall) to begin dealing the drugs directly to their network of friends and keeping the full profit for themselves.

Rare is the teen who enters a formal recovery program who doesn't have a court date and/or a probation officer. The quicker you can take action and pressure your child to stop participating in these risky behaviors, the better the chance that they won't end up with a criminal record.

Long showers

"So that's what they're doing in there." Most dads *think* they know why their sons' showers get longer in adolescence. If only it was that "innocent." Teens taking long showers often are using drugs while in the bathroom. It's probably the one "safe place" in your house where your child feels protected from being discovered. Even smoking drugs can be masked with the steam and noise of a hot shower.

Check this one out however you can.

Mask their behavior

Does your kid come home with a strong smell of cologne or perfume? "C'mon guys," your son will say. "Girls hang out with us too." Or, your daughter will tell you, "These boys were messing around with some of that Axe spray and spraying it all over each other. I got some on me too."

Or maybe they always have mints and gum in their pockets, and probably a fresh stick in their mouths when they get home. Heading straight to the bathroom to brush their teeth once they're home is another sign. All are common tactics to mask the odor of drugs or alcohol.

Steal

Teen drug abusers rarely have jobs, but they need money to continue their habits.

At this point, it is recommended that you buy a safe for your home, so you and your spouse can keep jewelry, credit cards, cash, prescription drugs, and other valuables locked up. Teens will search your home, even your bedroom, to find cash or something they can sell. If your son or daughter can't bring themselves to do it, their drug buddies will have no such reservations.

Shoplifting is common as well. If your teen is caught, let them suffer the consequences and don't give in to your desire to fix it to avoid a police record. Don't believe their story that it was on a dare or just a one-time thing.

Also don't believe it when they just happen to "find" an iPod or other gadget that you know you didn't buy them. Make sure it is returned to where they got it, even if it is to a lost and found collection.

On the other hand when the video games, iPods, cell phones or other high-value electronics you've given them are "lost", your teen may have begun to sell them to raise cash, either to buy drugs for themselves, or for seed money to begin dealing.

Threaten violence against you or themselves – or even suicide

As you close down on them with heavier consequences, it is a common tactic for your child to try to intimidate you or pronounce, "I'm just going to commit suicide." They know this is the ultimate hot button for you: no parent can imagine losing a child. Once again, they will surprise you with what they do to get you to back off and continue getting their way.

Never give in to any demand or threat like this, which will only reinforce the behavior. Instead, you should treat these threats seriously and act immediately. Follow through by calling 911 or getting them transported to the hospital for evaluation. That way you can feel assured your child's behavior and state of mind are evaluated by a professional. And if they are only idle threats, you can nip this behavior in the bud.

The majority of teens, who are using these threats to manipulate you, will quickly get the message that it doesn't work. Believe me, getting hauled off in handcuffs or to a psych ward for 72 hours of confinement and evaluation is not something they will want to experience again.

Become part of the Rave scene (Primary source: FBI)

"Raves" are high energy, all-night dances that often feature pounding techno music and flashing laser lights. Raves are found in most metropolitan areas and, increasingly, in rural areas throughout the country. The parties are held in permanent dance clubs, abandoned warehouses, empty buildings, or open fields, many times in remote locations. Teens will sometimes go to a publicized location first, then get directions to the final location.

Raves are usually advertised as safe and "drug and alcohol free" parties that are carefully supervised. The Rave culture is idealized as one of love and tolerance, reflected in the Ravers motto: Peace, Love, Unity, and Respect (PLUR).

In reality, Raves are dangerously over-crowded parties where your child can be exposed to rampant drug use and a high-crime environment. Numerous overdoses are documented at these events.

Also an unfortunate reality is that these events are anything but a display of tolerance and love, especially when it comes to you, the parent. They are actually just another way to push off any responsibility for bad and illegal behavior, and to continue getting high. I know this first hand after listening to a mother in one of my groups retell her story of being treated to a group chant of "F*** you bitch!" when she went looking for her runaway son at a Rave.

For Ravers, Methylenedioxymethamphetamine (MDMA, MDM) – Ecstasy for short – is the drug of choice. Other "club drugs" are frequently distributed as well. Club drugs include MDMA, GHB, and Rohypnol (also known as the "date rape" drugs), Ketamine (special K), Methamphetamine (aka "Meth"), and LSD. (See capsule descriptions of these drugs in **Chapter 6 - Drug Information**.)

Remember when you hear arguments about how safe Ecstasy is, or how many precautions Rave organizers may be taking, that these arguments are totally misguided. It's a drug party. The need to rely on artificial chemicals for happiness and peacefulness, is a wrong and dangerous long-term strategy.

Well-adjusted people, particularly those living in sobriety, learn that you can live life as it comes: good, bad, happy or sad. You don't need to mask every feeling or chase constant happiness. And in the end, that leads to a much more fulfilling life than a false "ecstasy" in pill form.

There are a ton of websites devoted to the promotion of Raving. Be on the lookout for these sites showing up on your computer history. And go there yourself for additional education so you can keep your teen away from the seductive and dangerous Rave scene.

See **Chapter 6 - Drug Information** for more detail on Raving, the associated drugs, and how to tell if your teen might be involved.

Chapter 4 - How You'll Feel

FOG – Fear, Obligation, and Guilt – is a common focus of psychotherapy. First popularized by Dr. Susan Forward in her book "Emotional Blackmail", it was originally applied to anyone dealing with a loved one who has a personality disorder. It certainly applies just as well to you in the case of your drug-using teen.

Therapists spend countless hours trying to instill behaviors that supplant these powerful influences on your mind. Nothing you do should be based on these three emotions, yet they play heavily on the minds of parents of teen drug abusers.

Fear

Here are some common fears you'll feel and some advice on each:

- *All the other parents I know have wonderful kids doing wonderful things. I can't share the truth about what's going on with my child, I'll be too embarrassed.* Of course you don't want to open up to everyone about your teen's problem, but building a support network is a key to surviving and being successful in getting help for your child. Choose people you can trust and share with them what's going on. You'll be surprised that most people will show compassion toward you. They all have their issues too. And for those friends, co-workers, and family members who judge you instead, they aren't the people you need in your life right now anyway.

- *I can't discipline my child any more strongly or I might lose my relationship with them.* Again, this is probably the toughest feeling to overcome for families dealing with teen drug abuse and the resulting defiant behavior. Problem teens will try and try again to wear you down so much that you will give in and give them more freedom to do what they want to do. After a week, or even a few days, many parents want so badly to rebuild the loving, trusting relationship they want with their child that they will begin to return privileges and freedom to their teen. What you need to remember is that your child will soon take advantage of any leeway you give them. And most importantly, ask yourself this question: What kind of relationship do I really have with my child? Is it one of integrity, mutual respect, and love? Or has their manipulation worn down your standards so much that you are letting the inmate run the asylum? Don't be afraid to be a parent and set boundaries and rules that you know are best for you child. Believe it or not, someday they'll thank you for it. See more on this topic in **Chapter 7 - How To Deal With Suspected Drug Use**.

- *My child is a really good athlete/musician/dancer. That's one of the positive things they have in their lives. I don't want to take that from them, or have them get into trouble or attend counseling that could interrupt their practice and participation schedule. They might have a future in this.* First, teens need to feel the consequences of their actions. You should not shield them from one of the most valuable lessons anyone can learn: mess up and you will feel the impact on your life. You should not be making excuses to coaches or teachers to cover up your teen's behavior. Sports or arts organizations have rules on conduct and drug use, so they shouldn't be allowing a teen who is using to participate anyway. The bottom line here is to think about what's more important, your teen living a happy, healthy long-term life, or a few years of "glory" on the court, field, or stage? If others are telling you that your teen has a drug or alcohol problem, or if you know in your gut that something is wrong, give up this fear and do what is best for your child's life.

- *What if my child hurts himself, or worse?* Remember what you learned in **Chapter 3 - What Your Teen Will Do**. First, that this is most often just an idle threat to get you to back off on discipline, and second, that you treat these threats seriously. If it's real, you'll get help. If not, they'll back down when they know they're going to be dealt with by the police or a visit to a psychiatric hospital.

- *Maybe I am over-reacting. After all, everyone does it.*
  The same Monitoring the Future study cited in the introduction found that slightly less than 50% of high school seniors reported using drugs of any kind at any time in their life. Obviously not "everyone" does it. As you read more of this book, the dangers of drug use will become apparent. And we won't know for years what the effects on the brain will be from the far more potent brand of pot now available to your teen. I predict it will be dire, with new evidence already showing potential psychosis brought on by regular use. Don't be sidetracked by the fear that this is just another "phase."

Obligation: I don't want to "give up" on them – I can fix this

When you feel this way, go back and review what this book tells you about how to deal with drug use by your teen. There, you'll find the step by step process you need to follow to discourage their behavior and send the clearest of messages that you don't approve. If you work at those steps for months – more likely years – and still don't get results, that in no way can be considered giving up on your child.

This feeling should be pointed directly back to teaching from Al Anon, the support group for those who have an alcoholic or addict family member: the three C's. You didn't **cause** their addiction, you can't **control** it, and you can't **cure** it.

What you'll do by continuing to give them more chances and attempting again and again to fix your child on your own, is really enabling their behavior. Remember what we've told you about the manipulation skills of teen users? They will reach for this "I can fix-it" button again and again because they know how much power it holds over parents.

Once you've cranked up the consequences without success, all the reasoning, discussion, second chances, and trust only serve to provide your child with greater opportunity to harm themselves and screw up their life, and yours.

You can't police your child into stopping their use. There's not any amount of shielding them from legal issues, badgering them to get their school work done, or rewards for good behavior that can control their abuse. Once your child's brain and body is altered by using drugs or alcohol that instills cravings for those substances, you can't cure their disease.

Resorting to hard-line, tough love tactics is just the next step in the progression. It's a tough lesson to learn, no doubt. But many who've stepped past their natural, protective urges have found that it is ultimately the best thing they could ever do for their child.

Guilt: What did I do wrong?

A lot of times when I first see parents, there's a lot of guilt associated with what they're going through. We need to eliminate that guilt from the process and learn that it's not what you've done, and move towards how we make it better. With teens, you're the Denial Buster. We need to be in the business of shaking them up. Saying clearly to them that they have a problem and that it won't be tolerated.

It's important for you to understand that, except in the very extreme cases of neglect or abuse on the part of parents, it's not your actions that cause your teen to use. It's almost the luck of the draw, and not necessarily that you put them in the wrong school, didn't spend enough time with her, got a divorce, or let him hang out with "bad" friends.

To be effective in treating the problem, you need to move past "mom did this" or "dad did that." I get a lot of this, "Don't tell my husband, but if he would have just done this differently, none of this would have happened." Remember this is a family disease. Every person has a component, but no one thing or person is definitely the cause of the drug use.

I'll get them into psychological counseling to help them find the *real* cause of their drug abuse

Counseling can achieve some benefits as part of a treatment plan, but we highly recommend seeing a specialist in addictive behaviors. See

Chapter 7 - How to Deal With Suspected Drug Use for a longer discussion of this topic.

I need to get him or her into a new environment

Many of you will be thinking these thoughts:

If I can just get 'em…

- away from their "bad" friends they'll make new friends who'll be a better influence on them.
- into a job so that they don't have as much free time to hang out.
- through high school so they can get past this phase and keep options like college open to them, so they can be successful in life.
- to college where they will get out of this negative environment, mature, and get busy with studies and other activities with a new group of better friends.
- into the military where they will have no choice, except to learn discipline, develop a work ethic, and stop their slacker behavior.

You think that by changing their environment, that they can start doing positive things and get away from their destructive behaviors.

Are you still denying that your child *is* one of the "bad friends" – thinking they are a victim of peer pressure instead of the reality that they seek others who will support their behavior and using? Do you really think a college campus or a work place with other teens is a great place to get them away from using drugs and alcohol? Do you think the discipline of the military can counter-balance the fact that plenty of soldiers and sailors on leave generally regard great prowess in alcohol consumption as a positive thing?

Teens don't just decide to stop using or get distracted enough to get better on their own. In reality, you'll just have the same teen, with the same issues, in a new environment. And many times their using will get worse.

He/She is doing much better. I want to show them I trust them again.

Your desire to get your family back to "normal" as soon as possible is completely natural. You want to restore peace in the home and, most of all, stop the conflict between you and your teen. You want that positive, loving, fun relationship that you always imagined you'd have with your kids.

Once you have disciplined your teen and doled out consequences for what they've been doing, you may begin to see some positive change in their behavior. This is a critical point in the process of dealing with your child, yet most parents make the mistake of restoring privileges and trust too soon.

At this point, when you find yourself saying things like the following, check yourself and hold back the desire to think you've made any dramatic change in a short time:

- It's been a really good week. They're doing much better in school and their attitude has been much better.
- He's been clean for two weeks now and I'm really proud of him.
- She went to school every day since the new semester began (Six, seven, eight days now?)

Think about the length of time your teen has been abusing drugs and alcohol. About how long they've been manipulating and lying to you. Think about the things they've done to *earn* your mistrust. And think again about the dangers of what they've been doing. Then think rationally about how fast that bad behavior can truly be changed.

This is the most important time to keep the pressure on. It's not the time to start giving them more freedom to go out and be with friends or get cell phone or car privileges restored.

Anyone can fake it for a week or two, and most will, in hopes that you'll back down enough to let them get back to what they want to do. Your teen knows you're tired of the arguments and from the effort of the 7/24 fight you have to wage to get them to change their behavior. They know if they give you just a little love and hope, you're dying to throttle back and take a break from it all.

So keep checking up on them, keep them restricted to school and home, and wait to see some true change over many weeks or months before they even begin to earn back any trust.

I know kids who've got six months or a year in long-term recovery programs and their parents still don't completely trust them. That's because those parents have enough experience with this whole process to know how kids behave, and what it takes to get human beings to truly change and begin living a different way.

This is a time when you can relieve yourself of making this judgment by working with a professional. Let the pro use his or her experience to listen to and observe your teen, then make these decisions when they see the beginnings of real behavior modification on the part of your child.

It takes time, and you need to resist your urge to react too soon to any positive signs. Stay strong, stay proactive, and see your new way of dealing with your teen through to get the best result for everyone.

Chapter 5 - The Mind of the Teen Drug User

What causes my teen to use?

Everyone has an opinion on what causes teens to begin using drugs, but it's a question that really can't be directly answered by one specific reason. And, in fact, in my years of counseling, I haven't found it to be that useful to try to find the cause.

Between family issues, school issues, peer pressure, addiction trends in the family and psychological makeup, there are many influences and many factors. Frequently it's a mix of factors – two percent of this and two percent of that – and it changes from person to person.

Every once in a while a teen will ask the question: why do I like drugs so much, or why do I drink to an excess? But in general, it's not important for the treatment process to know why. Maybe surprisingly, even kids in treatment are really not that interested in finding a "cause."

One of the basic tenants of the most prolific alcoholism/addiction family support groups, Al-Anon (www.al-anon.alateen.org), is that nothing but the disease itself causes the problem. The first of the organization's "Three C's" is, "I didn't cause my loved one's alcoholism [addiction]." Through 70 years of helping families of addicts and alcoholics, they have learned that the addiction is not caused through the action or inaction of any family member, spouse, or other person.

Certainly, there is a role in recovery for the teen to find out, "How did I get to this place?" Addicts especially have many character defects that they need to examine and overcome. But that is an issue for longer term self-discovery and recovery.

So the answer to the question, while not so important for the kids, is important for you so you can get past this issue and on to supporting the recovery of your teen. Go back to **Chapter 4 - How You'll Feel**, for more on this topic.

The differences between experimentation and addiction

Many times the answer here is something only time will tell. As you enter the world of drug use and recovery, you'll often hear "it's a process." Unfortunately for you and your family, most often you have to let your teen's life play out for some time, no matter how rough the road gets. Prepare yourself for a lot of ups and downs, over months, or maybe years. Though we all would like immediate answers, there usually are no shortcuts.

There are clinical answers to this question of "is he/she really an addict." The American Psychiatric Association publishes a manual called Diagnostic and Statistical Manual of Mental Disorders (DSM). This manual, part of any qualified counselor's training, contains a series of questions and criteria that are a guide to mental disease, including addiction.

According to the DSM-IV manual, here is the clinical definition for Substance Abuse: "A maladaptive pattern of substance use, leading to clinically significant impairment or distress, as manifested by one (or more) of the following occurring within a 12-month period."

The four abuse criteria:

1. Recurrent substance use resulting in a failure to fulfill major role obligations at work, school, or home (such as repeated absences or poor work performance related to substance use; substance-related absences, suspensions, or expulsions from school; or neglect of children or household).

2. Recurrent substance use in situations in which it is physically hazardous (such as driving an automobile or operating a machine when impaired by substance use).

3. Recurrent substance-related legal problems (such as arrests for substance related disorderly conduct).

4. Continued substance use despite having persistent or recurrent social or interpersonal problems caused or exacerbated by the effect of the substance (for example, arguments with spouse [parents] about consequences of

intoxication and physical fights).

According to the book, here is the clinical definition for Substance Dependence: "A maladaptive pattern of substance use, leading to clinically significant impairment or distress, as manifested by three (or more) of the following [seven criteria], occurring at any time in the same 12-month period."

The seven dependence criteria:

1. Tolerance as defined by either of the following: (a) A need for markedly increased amounts of the substance to achieve intoxication or the desired effect or (b) Markedly diminished effect with continued use of the same amount of the substance.

2. Withdrawal, as manifested by either of the following: (a) The characteristic withdrawal syndrome for the substance or (b) The same (or closely related) substance is taken to relieve or avoid withdrawal symptoms.

3. The substance is often taken in larger amounts or over a longer period than intended.

4. There is a persistent desire and unsuccessful attempts to cut down or control substance use.

5. A great deal of time is consumed in activities to obtain the substance, use the substance, or recover from its effects.

6. Important social, occupational [academic], or recreational activities are given up or reduced because of substance use.

7. The substance use is continued despite knowledge of having a persistent physical or psychological problem that is likely to have been caused or exacerbated by the substance (for example, current cocaine use despite recognition of cocaine-induced depression or continued drinking despite recognition that an ulcer was made worse by alcohol consumption).

While the factors in the APA manual are things I look at, I prefer not to diagnose people, especially teens, with that type of criteria of addiction. I find that normal conversations over time can provide an equally valuable sense of what a teen is doing. It also lets the teen discover answers for themselves about how they're managing their life, making good or bad choices, and overall level of satisfaction with their lives. Self-discovery will be much more meaningful to your teen compared to asking a few simple questions and returning a medical diagnosis.

What I've also found over the years, is that a diagnosis doesn't really have a bearing on what a counselor needs to do. Whether the teen is a full-blown addict or just using, doesn't really change the game plan.

Nevertheless, a qualified counselor can provide information to you on how to tell the difference between drug abuse and addiction.

Any teen with a number of negative issues stemming from drug use is in need of help. As a result of action on your part, often the non-addict (normie) can quit using and those issues will begin to improve. Even in relapse, they can brush themselves off and recognize the mistake, still go to school the next day, still improve their behavior at home, and even continue to follow through on heavier consequences such as legal issues.

A teen who's not addicted will generally say, "This isn't worth it. I'm always fighting with my parents, I have to stay home, I lost my car...I just don't want to do this." Those kids probably don't have true addictions.

For kids afflicted with addiction, that sound reasoning doesn't happen. Once they use, all other aspects of their lives spiral down around them. Even major consequences such as DUIs or felony charges such as theft, possession, assault, or dealing won't persuade them. Going to college, the car, the cell phone, a job, participation in sports; losing it all is not motivation to quit.

This lack of caring for any other aspect of their life is one of the key differences between a truly addicted teen versus a teenager who's going a little overboard with their experimentation. When consequences, restrictions, and loss of possessions don't have an effect, and when your child continues to escalate their bad behavior and drug use, that indicates that they are an addict. And addicts cannot be cured by you or the addict.

The physical symptoms of the teen drug user

A number of symptoms in your child could indicate drug use, rather than actual medical problems. Of course, consult a physician should your child tell you about any of the following symptoms. Ask your doctor to help you sort out developing sickness or disease from what might be caused by the affects of drugs.

Setting aside behavioral symptoms, here are some physical symptoms that should be a red flag for you, especially if your teen has never had any similar problems in the past:

- Constant fatigue, sleepiness, or drowsiness
- Red eyes and/or blurred vision needing frequent eye drops
- Restlessness, inability to sit still, shaking or twitching
- Breathing problems, asthma-like symptoms
- Weight loss
- Frequent stomach pain and/or vomiting
- Nutrition deficiencies which often show up as bad skin or deteriorating dental health
- Heart racing, chest hurting
- Kidney infections
- Blood in urine.

Why addiction is a disease

Though many people have a hard time accepting that alcoholism and/or addiction is a disease, you will most likely be convinced by your child's counterintuitive and irrational behavior. You should know that they don't really care any less about their life, it's just that they can't help themselves.

Because you're not an addict, you can walk away from the next drink or drug (If you are one, then you get it.). Addicts exhibit behavior quite different from the rest of us and we list a sampling of them here:

- Overwhelming curiosity about how each drug will make them feel under its influence
- Inability to leave any alcohol unconsumed or drug unused
- Cravings for the next high at all times

- Lack of care about the consequences of using
- Using to feel better, not just for social reasons
- Compulsion to do everything to excess, not just drugs
- Inability to learn from life troubles, obvious health risks, and harm experienced by others who use and abuse drugs
- Irrational reasoning and justification of their use.

Medical experts have found that as a person uses drugs over time, the function of the brain shifts. At first, the drug triggers pleasure centers in the brain, but over time, the brain instead begins to seek to avoid the pain and discomfort of withdrawal when the substance is absent. The brain actually changes its functioning to one where it expects the alcohol and/or drugs to be present, and among other things, sets up a strong craving when they are not. This altering in organ function is one of the definitions of a disease.

Accepting addiction as a disease is a key step for you in the recovery of your teen drug abuser. In fact, it is quite freeing to come to this realization. It will help you move past the blame, anger, hurt, and confusion, and on to action and treatment of this literally life-threatening condition that is afflicting your child.

Can young teens turn their lives around, or are they too immature to realize they need help?

Research has shown how differently a teen brain functions. It is known that at around ages 10 to 13 years, the brain is pruning back neuro pathways mostly developed in humans as very young children. The changes are one of the most intense periods of brain development. Some in the neuroscience field liken this period in the brain to the phrase "use it or lose it." What the child is focused on and active in at this stage is what is going to be retained. Good stuff in, good stuff out. Garbage in, garbage out. Addictive behaviors in…you get the point.

In addition, a group of researchers at McLean Hospital in Belmont, Mass. found that a completely different part of the brain is engaged by teens as they view the world. Where adult brains use the frontal cortex, brain scans from the study group of 10 to 18 year-olds showed the amygdala lighting up. That's important because the frontal cortex is a more rational part of the brain, while the amygdala is associated with gut reactions, impulsivity, and risk-taking.

The story, *The Teen Brain: It's Just Not Grown Up Yet*, from National Public Radio's Richard Knox, says the process continues throughout the teenage years.

What could be a more perfect environment for saying "let's do it," ignoring the long term risks, and building drug habits?

Obviously, the older people get, the more life experience they accumulate, and the wiser they become. While there does not seem to be a consensus on when the brain is considered "mature," it is thought that the male adult brain continues to grow until the age of 24 or 25, so physiologically, there is not a full development of the personality in the teen years. Not to say that a 24 year old is wise either!

With girls the maturation usually takes place a little younger. Girls typically are a lot more difficult, and much more savvy. This question is more difficult to answer for females because their reasons for using tend to be different from males. Usually family factors are much more prevalent, rather than pure recreation on the male side. If you have a girl who's really out of control, really high risk and involved in drugs, guys, sneaking out – there are often some serious family or personal issues in play.

If I ask kids where they see themselves in five years, they don't have clear plans. Most teens just don't have that ability yet. They live in the moment; in a world of instant gratification from video games, television, and – for the most part – have a very comfortable life with very little effort. The on-demand escape and good feelings they get from drugs and alcohol feed right into that lifestyle.

Despite these issues of immaturity, there is hope for younger teens. Some do have the ability to recognize that the drug-using lifestyle isn't the way to go. The things they're doing make them happy in the moment, but not in hindsight (even for addicts). They can look ahead and see that working hard now will pay off later. They figure out that if they don't finish high school, they don't have much of a life to look forward to. I have worked with kids as young as 13 to 14 years old who've hit a bottom like this.

In fact, kids this young are generally still in the experimentation stage. They may well have moved beyond pot to heavy drugs like prescription meds and even heroin. But most times they have not developed a physical dependency on any drug and are typically able to kick the habit a little easier. While we do see a trend where kids are getting introduced to drugs at a much younger age, they can also more quickly get to a point where they want to quit and don't want to continue the problems in their life that drugs cause.

With older kids of 15, 16, and up you do see addiction kicking in. They might also want to quit, but by then the task is much more difficult, even impossible, without professional help.

Play it by ear, and manage your expectations. No matter what they are involved in and how dangerous some of their behaviors are, they're still a kid, and may not be able to rationally approach the problem. They are still going through the maturation process. However, there are individuals who don't have to go through residential treatment, or even IOP, to get better.

One big lesson here is: Don't wait to start dealing with this problem. Start when you first see these behaviors beginning so you and your child will have a better chance of putting a stop to it.

Chapter 6 - Drug Information

Rather than a list of individual drugs, we feel it is more valuable to categorize the drugs into how they are used – or abused. This way you get the information you need to recognize the evidence that users leave behind. This information will enable you to detect your teens' drug use and to begin to see his or her level of involvement through the type of drugs being used. The exact drug of choice is less important.

In general, think about what to look for in this way: If you were getting high using a particular drug, and based on what you know about taking the drug, what items around the house would you use?

More drug information and images

Many of the descriptions in this section come from the National Institute on Drug Abuse. For more detailed information, visit the NIDA website (www.nida.nih.gov). The NIDA website has a very comprehensive, well-organized database on drugs, so there is no need for us to re-create that in this book.

About NIDA

The NIDA mission is to lead the Nation in bringing the power of science to bear on drug abuse and addiction though two critical components:

- Strategic support and conduct of research across a broad range of disciplines.
- Ensuring the rapid and effective dissemination and use of the results of that research to significantly improve prevention, treatment, and policy as it relates to drug abuse and addiction.

To find out what any type of pill or drug looks like, just use Google Images and search for the drug you are looking for.

Smoked Drugs

The evidence you'll find:

- Pipes or bongs made from glass, soda bottles/cans or water bottles (from small to the 5-gallon variety)
- Home-made bong or pipe components (often appearing burnt with resulting soot residue left behind)
- Tin foil, brillo pad bits, or screens removed from faucets or cut from windows (needed for keeping burning drugs from being inhaled in a pipe)
- Emptied marker pens
- PVC lawn sprinkler pipe
- Cast iron plumbing pipe
- Apples or other fruit
- Just about anything you can imagine stuffing with the drug and sucking smoke from
- Bong water, a foul smelling, dark brown residue left from smoking marijuana, often discarded in water bottles
- Any sort of smooth, glass basin such as a light bulb with the screw-in end broken off
- Cutoff bottoms of soda cans
- Tin foil with black lines (almost looks like felt-tip pen marks) that are left on it from melting powderized drugs from a heat source underneath to vaporize and inhale the drug
- Heat sources such as lighters, candles, or even gas torches
- Metal hose clamps, citrus zesters, and other tools that are used to grate pills into powder
- Niacin (elongated pink pills) used to flush THC from the body prior to drug tests
- Deodorizers, gum, mints, eye drops for masking use
- Dryer fabric softener sheets to mask the smell of the smoke as they exhale

- Black smudges or fingerprints on furniture, walls, doors, and other surfaces around the house from smoking residue on hands
- Burnt fingers

Notes:
1. No one smokes tobacco out of a bong
2. A "Hookah" is a water pipe that is used to smoke a variety of flavored tobaccos. They are completely legal and hookah bars are popular among young adults. However, this behavior can be used to mask the smell of other smoked drugs and sometimes is a warning sign of other smoking.

Drugs ingested in this way:

Marijuana

Slang: Pot, weed, grass, ganga, and many, many others

Green, brown, or gray mixture of dried, shredded leaves, stems, seeds, and flowers of the hemp plant (*Cannabis sativa*).

The most commonly used illegal drug in the U.S. The main active chemical is THC.

More info

Short-term effects include memory and learning problems, distorted perception, lack of motivation, increased appetite, and difficulty thinking and solving problems.

THC can be detected by standard urine testing methods several days after smoking, but in heavy, chronic users, traces can be detected for up to 30 days after stopping use.

Heroin

Slang: Smack, H, ska, junk

Heroin usually appears as a white or brown powder or as a black sticky substance, known as "black tar heroin" (rare among teens).

More info

Heroin is an opiate drug that is synthesized from morphine, a naturally occurring substance extracted from the seed pod of the opium poppy plant.

Often thought of as an injected drug, most young users begin by smoking heroin fumes created by heating the powder on a metal or glass surface. Usually only advanced heroine users inject the drugs with hypodermic needles.

Short-term effects include a surge of euphoria followed by alternately wakeful and drowsy states ("on the nod") and cloudy mental functioning. With regular heroin use, tolerance develops and more heroin is needed to achieve the same intensity of effect.

PCP

Slang: Angel dust, ozone, wack, rocket fuel, and others

White crystalline powder readily soluble in water or alcohol with a distinctive bitter chemical taste. PCP can be mixed easily with dyes and is often sold on the illicit drug market in a variety of colored powder forms.

Rare in high schools, not cheap, not a good high. More often used by criminal element because of rage, numbness, and extraordinary strength it delivers.

More info

Phencyclidine was developed in the 1950s as an intravenous anesthetic. Its use has since been discontinued due to serious adverse effects.

For smoking, PCP is often applied to a leafy material such as mint, parsley, oregano, or marijuana. Depending upon how much and by what route PCP is taken, its effects can last approximately 4 to 6 hours.

Pharmaceuticals

See below for properties of these drugs.

More info

Rather than swallowing prescription drugs, users often crush or grate them into powder form, then heat them to create vapor that they inhale. This provides a higher dose more quickly than a pill can deliver.

New trends in smoked drugs

Salvia

Salvia divinorum recently gained notoriety when a well known teen celebrity was captured on video smoking it from a bong.

People in the Oaxaca region of Mexico, where the plant is native, originally brewed a tea using juice from leaves or chewed the leaves directly, but kids will most often smoke a dried leaf preparation in a water pipe or bong.

Since the untreated dry leaf produces unnoticeable or only light effects, the drug is sold in concentrated preparations. This fortified preparation is labeled as 2x, 5x, etc., based on how concentrated the leaves are. The drug is sold by the gram in concentrations from 2x to 100x, with the price ranging from about $10/gram to $70/gram for the most potent.

Most often called by its genus name Salvia, this drug is also known as Diviner's Sage, María Pastora, and Seer's sage. Being a psychoactive plant, it produces a fast, short-lived hallucinogenic high. The active drug in Salvia creates dissociative and delirium effects including visions and hallucinations. But users report recovering quickly, so it is sometimes called the "working man's high" because it can be smoked or ingested on a lunch break and the user will return to a relatively normal state within 15 to 20 minutes.

The effects of the active elements in Salvia produce the hallucinations mentioned and also a euphoric effect, since the drug induces the same reaction in the brain as many anti-depressant drugs. Though the substance is said to be inherently dysphoric, which means it can also cause a depressed, sad mood, research reports say only a few users report this side effect.

One complicating factor in combating its use is that it is still legal in most countries, most U.S. states, and is not regulated by U.S. federal drug laws. At this writing it was illegal in 13 states, while most state governments were at least considering bans, or making the sale of Salvia illegal to minors, as it is in California and Maine. Search Wikipedia for "Salvia" to get the latest status on legality in your state.

Though we don't have studies to prove it, at least one of the recovering addicts we interviewed said that teens don't favor Salvia because it is a fairly high-cost drug, with a very short high. Prescription drugs and marijuana are cheaper and produce longer lasting highs. The only benefits to drug users are that it usually won't show on a drug test and is legal in many areas.

Salvia may have the reputation of being a safe, quick high, but since it affects the k-opioid receptor in the brain, strongly implicated as an integral neurochemical component of addiction, that simply is not true.

A recent web search for "buy salvia" returned 503,000 results and there are dozens of sites selling it on the Internet. Check your teen's browsing history for any URL with "salvia" in it, since selling sites virtually all include the word in their domain names.

So keep an eye out for this one, which has plenty of popularity. The 2011 NIH "Monitoring the Future Study" showed that the percentage of seniors using Salvia is ahead of Oxycontin, ecstasy, cocaine, and inhalants.

Spice

Spice is a drug that seems to be the latest fad among teens. I am seeing kids who are using it all the time now, compared to almost no mention just months ago. Spice and its variants can be purchased at smoke shops and online.

Also known as K2 (other names are sure to catch on such as Genie and Happy Smoke), Spice was created as a synthetic marijuana by lacing leafy herbs or incense with one or more drug compounds that produce a similar effect to the THC in marijuana. The primary compound is called JWH-018, but that's really beside the point. The whole point of Spice is to sidestep the illegality of marijuana.

As of the end of 2011, this new drug can't be detected by standard, in-home drug tests. But the drug has become a problem in U.S. military forces, with several large busts recently in the news. With the government focused on the problem and backing it with money to develop a test, we should see one soon.

Since it is made to be a synthetic marijuana, smoking is the preferred way to use this drug. See Smoked Drugs in this chapter for more information.

Clinical studies at the Medical College of Virginia found that the active ingredient in Spice does its job with three to five times the potency of THC. And it has a very strong preference for attaching to the brain and spinal cord receptors that produce the intoxicating effects of marijuana. Good for the therapeutic uses that may have been intended for JWH-018, but as usual, probably of even greater interest to drug abusers.

According to Home Health Testing, an online home health and home drug test business, "Unlike marijuana, synthetic cannabis does not have a signature smell. The high is relatively short (30 minutes or so) and generally shorter than a high from marijuana. So it is less likely you will catch someone "acting high" when they are using the drug. However, this may vary depending on the potency of the product consumed. The red-eyed look of someone high on marijuana can also be seen in someone high on Spice, as can the general slowness and subdued behavior."

Reports say that the new Spice fad had its origins in Kansas, Missouri, and Arizona. In news reports, Jeremiah Morris, a forensic scientist for the Johnson County Criminalistics Laboratory in Mission, Kansas, said the drug can cause increased heart rate, loss of consciousness, paranoia and, occasionally, psychotic episodes. As with all drugs, individuals have different reactions, but Morris added that users do not have to smoke excessive amounts of Spice to experience potentially harmful symptoms.

And if you want to hear from the horse's mouth on whether this is a "safe" alternative to weed, Clemson University Professor John Huffman, the person in charge of the studies that created JWH-018, was quoted as saying, "I emphasize that this compound was not designed to be a super-THC. It is simply one of many compounds synthesized by my group and others for the purpose of investigating the relationship between chemical structure and biological activity. It should absolutely NOT be used as a recreational drug."

Law enforcement has begun to shut down trade in this dangerous drug. On March 1, 2011, a national ban on JWH-018, JWH-073, JWH-200, CP 47,497, and CP 47,497 C8) was finally enacted in the U.S., declaring these chemicals to be Schedule I drugs—unsafe, highly abused substances with no legitimate medical use. In addition, at least 18 states have banned synthetic marijuana.

The University of Michigan study found that in 2011, 11.4% of high school seniors nationwide indicated using it in the prior 12 months, but the authors think that, since the substance is so new, next year's survey numbers will provide more accurate information on the use of Spice.

* * * * * *

Inhaled or "Huffed" Drugs

The evidence you'll find:
- Aerosols, solvents, or household cleaners that are used up quickly or no longer contain propellant:
  - Canned air dusters (such as used to clean or dust computers)
  - Whipped cream, deodorant, shaving cream
  - Spray paints, paint thinners or removers, degreasers, dry-cleaning fluids, gasoline, and lighter fluid
- Art or office supplies including correction fluids, felt-tip markers, electronic contact cleaners, and glue
- Bruises, facial cuts from falls (due to quick onset of effects)
- Balloons, bags.

Drugs ingested in this way:
Slang: Whippets, poppers, snappers

Breathable chemical vapors that users intentionally inhale because of the chemicals' mind-altering effects.

Along with pot, often one of the first drugs used among young teens.

More info

Substances inhaled are often common household products that contain volatile solvents or aerosols. Includes medical anesthetics such as ether, chloroform, halothane, and nitrous oxide. Also a class of inhalants called Nitrites, commonly known as "poppers." Often sold in small brown bottles labeled as video head cleaner, room odorizer, leather cleaner, or liquid aroma.

Very intense, short, cheap high. Inhalants can be breathed in through the nose or mouth in a variety of ways (huffing), such as sniffing or snorting fumes from a container, spraying aerosols directly into the nose or mouth, or placing an inhalant-soaked rag in the mouth. The intoxication produced by inhalants usually lasts just a few minutes; therefore, users often try to extend the "high" by continuing to inhale repeatedly over several hours.

* * * * * *

Snorted Drugs

The evidence you'll find:
- Knives or razor blades with film or deposit on it
- Flat hard surfaces – CD cases, CDs, mirrors, glass-framed wall art that have a residue or scratches on them
- Straws, emptied pen barrels or other thin, hollow tubes used for snorting or "tooting" the drug

Drugs ingested in this way:
Cocaine
Slang: Coke, snow, flake, blow
Snorted and sniffed, but also injected and smoked.
More info
Common in many high schools, especially in up-scale neighborhoods.

A powerfully addictive drug, cocaine usually makes the user feel euphoric and energetic. Common health effects include heart attacks, respiratory failure, strokes, and seizures. Large amounts can cause bizarre and violent behavior. In rare cases, sudden death can occur on the first use of cocaine or unexpectedly thereafter.

Ketamine

Slang: Special K, Vitamin K

An anesthetic, mostly used in veterinary practice. Rare.

PCP

Slang: Angel dust, ozone, wack, rocket fuel, and many others

White crystalline powder readily soluble in water or alcohol with a distinctive bitter chemical taste.

More info

Rare among high school kids because it's not cheap and not the type of high they want. More often used by criminal element because of rage, numbness, and extraordinary strength it delivers.

Phencyclidine was developed in the 1950s as an intravenous anesthetic. Its use has since been discontinued due to serious adverse effects.

PCP can be mixed easily with dyes and the snorted version is often sold on the illicit drug market in a variety of colored powder forms.

Effects can last approximately 4 to 6 hours.

New trends in snorted drugs

Bath Salts

This new "designer" drug is another mostly-legal substance that drug users have discovered. The active drug here is called Methylenedioxypyrovalerone or MDPV, which is similar to meth and is also produced by "street chemists." Designer in this sense means that drug makers will continue to make new formulations of the drug, keeping them below the radar of law enforcement.

This is another case where the innocent sounding marketing name may entice kids who think this could be a safer choice for getting high.

However, this drug is not an actual salt you would ever use in a bath. The drug is only borrowing legitimacy from the Epsom salts you might use in the tub.

According to NIDA, the drugs are marketed through smoke shops under names like Ivory Wave, Purple Wave, Red Dove, Bolivian Bath, Blue Silk, Zoom, Cloud Nine, and a number of other ethereal sounding labels. To further deflect the law, these bath salts are typically labeled as "not for human consumption," but of course that's exactly what they are intended for.

Whatever the exact chemical makeup, the primary ingredients are extremely easy to overdose on. NIDA reported that within the first two months of 2011, there had already been 251 documented cases called into poison control centers, exceeding the 236 cases for all of 2010.

According to WebMD, this severe stimulant produces effects such as agitation, psychosis, and violence in users. High blood pressure, increased heart rate, chest pain, hallucinations, paranoia, and suicide are reported as side effects.

The drug is a powder so will typically be snorted or smoked, but could be injected as well. Look for the same evidence you would expect for other smoked drugs. Long term effects, such as addiction, are unknown because there is not enough of a long-term history of use.

Since the specific formulation of drugs like bath salts is a moving target, local and state legislators are moving quickly to make the ingredients illegal as they have for crystal meth, Spice, etc.

* * * * * *

Oral Drugs

The evidence you'll find:

- Over-the-counter (OTC) medicine packaging in unusual quantities in the trash

- Prescriptions missing, empty prescription bottles, or requests for refills of pain medicines given during recovery from injuries or surgery
- Baggies, scales, measuring devices for breaking up, measuring what they bought and sold
- Contents of OTC cold or vitamin capsules in the trash as users empty them for refilling with illegal substances
- See previous sections for additional evidence you'll find when prescription drugs are being abused by crushing and smoking them

Drugs ingested in this way:

Prescriptions meds

Commonly abused classes of prescription drugs include opioids (often prescribed to treat pain), central nervous system depressants (often prescribed to treat anxiety and sleep disorders), and stimulants (prescribed to treat narcolepsy, ADHD, and obesity).

Also frequently smoked or snorted.

More info

Lock up and keep track of any prescription and over the counter meds you have. When your teen is given a legitimate prescription for these drugs, do not give them the whole bottle of pills. Keep it secure and give your child only what they need, as they need it, then watch them take it.

When a legitimate prescription is required, ask your doctor to write it for only 10 or a dozen pills, rather than more than you probably will ever use. If you do have extras, contact law enforcement to see how you can properly dispose of them. Flushing down the toilet is not a proper way to do it.

Commonly used:
- Opioids include oxycodone (OxyContin, Percocet, Percodan, Tylox), propoxyphene (Darvon), hydrocodone (Vicodin),

hydromorphone (Dilaudid), meperidine (Demerol), and diphenoxylate (Lomotil)

- Central nervous system depressants include barbiturates such as pentobarbital sodium (Nembutal), and benzodiazepines such as diazepam (Valium), and alprazolam (Xanax)
- Stimulants include dextroamphetamine (Dexedrine) and methylphenidate (Ritalin), adderall
- Clonidine (Catapres) is used to treat hypertension (high blood pressure). Although not approved by the FDA for these purposes, Clonidine has also been used to relieve alcohol withdrawal, as an aid in methadone and opiate detoxification, as an aid in quitting smoking.

LSD

Slang: Acid, blotter

Two forms: tabs or liquid (very rare)

LSD in liquid form is dropped onto sheets, with each tab (dose) ¼ size of a stamp with a logo on it. A sheet has roughly 100-150 tabs, with some type of stamp that is the logo of the supplier.

More info

Each tab is $10-30, so not likely that kids are selling or possessing so much that you will find the liquid form.

Unpredictable psychological effects. With large enough doses, users experience delusions and visual hallucinations. Physical effects include increased body temperature, heart rate, and blood pressure; sleeplessness; and loss of appetite.

MDMA

Slang: Ecstasy, X, XTC, X, Adam, hug, beans, love drug (Each brand also has its own slang name)

MDMA is a liquid that is the hallucinogenic compound in Ecstasy.

The pills have color variations and patterns, always with a stamp for the maker, but producers counterfeit especially popular brands.

More info

Ecstasy is a very popular drug among teens. It is cheap and easy to produce.

The common formulation includes MDMA and a stimulant such as caffeine, pseudoephedrine, or methamphetamine. Most low grade are mostly caffeine with a little MDMA. High grade ecstasy can contain cocaine.

Short-term effects include feelings of mental stimulation, emotional warmth, enhanced sensory perception, and increased physical energy. Adverse health effects can include nausea, chills, sweating, teeth clenching, lip chewing, muscle cramping, and blurred vision.

In bulk, the pills are $3 to $4 each, but "retail" for $20 to $25 per pill, so it is a very lucrative drug for dealers, all the way down to the high school kid who wants to make a little spending money.

Over-the-Counter Meds

Cough and cold medicines contain dextromethorphan (DXM), which can have beneficial effects when taken as recommended, but when abused can lead to serious adverse health consequences.

More info

DXM is the active ingredient found in OTC cough and cold medications. In order to experience the mind-altering effects of DXM, excessive amounts of liquid or gel caps must be consumed. Teens are the primary abuser because of the availability and accessibility of these products.

The effects vary with dose, ranging from a mild stimulant effect with distorted visual perceptions at low (approximately 2-ounce) doses to a sense of complete dissociation, being "out of body" and detached from their environment, at doses of 10 ounces or more.

In very large quantities, DXM can cause effects similar to those of ketamine and PCP because these drugs affect similar sites in the brain. These effects can include impaired motor function, numbness, nausea/vomiting, and increased heart rate and blood pressure.

Nyquil Cough is the one of the most common recreationally-used meds because it has both the DXM and Doxylamine (a sedative) without the stimulant acetaminophen.

Methamphetamine

Slang: Speed, meth, chalk, ice, crystal, glass

Methamphetamine is a white, odorless, bitter-tasting crystalline powder that easily dissolves in water or alcohol and is taken orally, intranasally (snorting), by needle injection, or by smoking.

More info

An addictive stimulant that is closely related to amphetamine, but has longer lasting and more toxic effects on the central nervous system. It has a high potential for abuse and addiction.

The drug increases wakefulness and physical activity and decreases appetite. Chronic, long-term use can lead to psychotic behavior, hallucinations, and stroke. Meth is highly toxic so use is usually associated with other internal organ problems.

In fact, it is so toxic that the smell of the chemical is often obvious on the skin of users.

Steroids

Slang: Roids, juice, sauce, slop

Mostly synthetic substances similar to the male sex hormone testosterone.

More info

Some people, especially athletes, abuse anabolic steroids to enhance performance and appearance. Abuse of anabolic steroids can lead to serious health problems, some of which are irreversible.

In males, adverse effects may include shrinking of the testicles and breast development. In females, adverse effects may include growth of facial hair, menstrual changes, and deepened voice. In teenagers, growth may be halted prematurely and permanently. Other adverse effects can include severe acne, high blood pressure and jaundice. In some rare cases liver and kidney tumors or even cancer may develop. Extreme mood swings can also occur, including manic-like symptoms that could lead to violence.

Another way to detect use is that abusers usually need a constant supply of pain pills – Tylenol, aspirin, Aleve – as well, because of muscle pain from the intense workouts that steroids enable.

Alcohol Remains One of the Most Abused Drugs

Remember the fact we presented right at the beginning of this book: 53.6 percent of the teens surveyed had consumed alcohol at least once. Alcohol is not to be dismissed as innocent or "less bad" than other drugs.

"The underage Drinking Epidemic," an article in the June 12, 2011 issue of *Parade*, reports that the Center for Disease Control says that 90% of teen drinking is done while binge drinking, a very dangerous and risky behavior. The article reports that emergency room physicians are seeing 200,000 adolescents visit the ER annually because of an excess of alcohol. And kids arrive with blood-alcohol levels in ranges from .35 to as high as .4, a level at which 50% of people die. They also say that just 10 years ago, they would see such blood-alcohol levels only in chronic alcoholics.

The goal now is to get as drunk as possible as fast as possible, so hard liquor is therefore favored over the low level of alcohol in most cheap beer. But who wants to taste what you're drinking? The goal is to use sweet, easy-to-drink beverages that can be consumed quickly and easily. The makers of sweet malt liquors and "alco-pops" are happy to accommodate adolescents who party this way.

Also Google "Jungle Juice" to get a taste of what's going on.

Don't ignore drinking or think it's more "OK" than doing drugs.

More on Ecstasy and the Rave Scene

Because many Rave drugs are colorless, odorless, and tasteless, they can be added without detection to beverages by individuals who want to intoxicate or sedate your teen in order to commit sexual assaults.

Rave promoters capitalize on the effects of club drugs. Bottled water and sports drinks are sold at Raves, often at inflated prices, to manage hyperthermia and dehydration. Cool down rooms are provided, usually at a cost, as a place to cool off due to the increased body temperature of the drug user.

A key indicator that your teen is part of the Rave scene is the brightly colored clothing and accessories favored by Ravers.

Rave wear is usually lightweight and loose-fitting, like bikini tops, tank tops, tube tops, and open-back halter tops. Ravers often dress in multiple layers so they can remove clothes as they become overheated from dancing for hours, and from the drugs they ingest. Clothing also includes costumes that match the Rave theme of the night.

Telltale Rave paraphernalia includes menthol nasal inhalers, surgical masks, chemical lights, and neon glow sticks to increase sensory perception and enhance the Rave experience. Accessories include neon-colored leggings, necklaces, and bracelets (sometimes made of pill-shaped candy), with bracelets worn in multiples running from the wrist up the forearm.

Specific accessories to be on the lookout for are lollipops and pacifiers, which Ravers use to prevent the involuntary teeth clenching and chewing of the inside of the cheeks or lips that Ecstasy induces. (In fact, in Northern England MDMA tablets are called Cowies because they make the user grind their teeth like a cow chewing its cud.) Pacifiers are often worn around the neck on plastic beaded necklaces.

The use of MDMA has spawned its own language. Notice how many terms on the following list romanticize use of the drug, alluding to a higher consciousness where peace and love for all abound.

Read on for a list of just some of the common Rave-related terms you should be aware of:

- MDMA names: Adam, B-bombs, Batmans, Beans, Blue kisses, Blue lips, Bibs, Candy, Charity, Chrystal methadrine, Clarity, Cristal (Spanish), Dead road, Debs, Decadence, Dex, Dexedrine, Diamonds, Disco biscuit, Doctor, Drivers, E, E-bombs, Essense, Exiticity, Fastin, Four leaf clover, Glaggler, Go, GWM, Happy drug, Happy pill, Herbal bliss, Hug drug, Jack n Jills, Jellies, Kleenex, Letter biscuits, Little one, Little fella, Love drug, Love pill, Love trip, Lover's speed, Lovers' special, Mellow Drug of America, Methedrine, Mini beans, Molly, Nineteen, Pollutants, Rave energy, Ritual spirit, Scooby snacks, Skittles, Slammin'/Slamming, Smarties, Snackies, Spivas, Strawberry shortcake, Swedgers, Sweeties, Tachas, Tens, Thiz, Tutus,

73

Tweety Birds, U.S.P., Ultimate Xphoria, Venus, Wafers, Wheels, Whiffledust, White dove, Wigits, X, X-ing, X-Pills, XTC.

- Banging tunes: loud tunes with a strong beat that sound especially good when on MDMA/Ecstasy
- Blueroom : Room at parties where revellers go to rest and chill-out
- Bumping up : MDMA combined with powder cocaine
- Cabbaged : intellectually impaired through excessive drug use
- Candy ravers : a raver highly adorned with beads and baubles
- Candyflipping on a string : Combining or sequencing LSD with MDMA; mixing LSD, MDMA, and cocaine
- Candy Raver : Young people who attend raves; rave attendees who wear candy jewelry
- Chilled tunes : tranquil music played later in the trip
- Chillout room : the room at parties where revelers go to rest
- Chocolate Chip Cookies : MDMA combined with heroin or methadone
- Coming up : starting to feel the effects of taking MDMA/Ecstasy
- Coming down : feeling the acute effects of taking MDMA/Ecstasy diminish
- Cuddle puddle : a clump or pile of Ecstasy users on the floor
- Domex : PCP and MDMA
- Dopey : MDMA/Ecstasy mixed with a depressant
- Double drop : take two tablets of MDMA simultaneously
- Dropping : swallowing an MDMA/Ecstasy pill
- Double stacked: MDMA/Ecstasy pill reputedly of twice standard potency
- E-puddle : A cuddle puddle (see above)
- E-tard : Person stupid or out-of-hand under the influence of MDMA (methylenedioxymethamphetamine)
- Elephant-flipping : Use of PCP and MDMA
- Flower : flipping Ecstasy (MDMA) mixed with mushrooms

74

- Foxy, Foxy methoxy : N,N-Diisopropyl-5-methoxytryptamine (5-MeO-DIPT)
- H - bomb : Ecstasy (MDMA) mixed with heroin
- Hammerheading : MDMA (methylenedioxymethamphetamine) used in combination with Viagra
- Hippie-flip : Use of mushrooms and MDMA (methylenedioxymethamphetamine)
- Hoop, Hooping, Plugging : Rectal administration of MDMA
- Hugs and Kisses : Combination of methamphetamine and MDMA
- Hydro : Amphetamine; high quality methamphetamine; marijuana; MDMA; marijuana grown in water (hydroponic)
- Kitty-flipping : Use of ketamine and MDMA
- Liquid Ecstasy : gamma-hydroxybutyrate (GHB)
- Methylendioxyamphetamine (MDA) ; MDMA
- Luved up, luvved up, luv'd up, luvdup : fully under the influence of MDMA/Ecstasy
- Mac Dre : a type of MDMA pill (from the California gangsta rapper Mac Dre)
- Mashed : state of mind after consumption of several pills of MDMA/Ecstasy
- Mitsubishis : brand of MDMA/Ecstasy (*also 007s, Armanis, Batmans, Bermuda triangles, Blue Nikes, Buddhas, Butterflies, Ferraris, Mercedes, Playboys, Pokemons, Red Devils, Red Stop Signs, Rolexes, Supermans, Volkswagons, White Diamonds, X-Files, Yin Yangs, etc.*)
- Nexus-flipping : Use of Nexus (2-CB) and MDMA
- NOX : Use of nitrous oxide and MDMA
- On A Mission : in search of MDMA/Ecstasy
- Parachuting : Crushing up an MDMA tablet, rolling it up in a tissue or thin napkin, and then swallowing them
- Peeper: MDMA user
- Pikachu : Pills containing PCP and Ecstasy

- Potatoed : under the influence of marijuana while coming down off MDMA
- Roll/rolling: under the influence of MDMA
- Sextasy : Ecstasy used with Viagra
- Sledging : coming down from MDMA/Ecstasy etc at five in the morning...
- Sorted : having arranged one's supply of MDMA/Ecstasy
- Speedy : MDMA/Ecstasy mixed with a stimulant
- Super X : Combination of methamphetamine and MDMA
- Totally spent : Hangover feeling that is an adverse effect of MDMA
- Thizz : Hyphy Slang for MDMA
- Thizzing : under the influence of MDMA
- Triple stacked: MDMA/Ecstasy pill reputedly of triple standard potency

* * * * * *

New Trends in Drug Use

More on prescriptions meds

In March 2010 the nation's emergency physicians issued a warning to parents about the dangers of prescription drug abuse, which is now the second leading class of abused drugs, after marijuana. The results of a recent survey showed that nearly three-quarters of a million people (741,425) needed emergency care in one year because of prescription drug abuse. Of more concern is that the survey reflects data from a couple of years ago, and the problem continues to grow.

In a news release from the American College of Emergency Physicians (ACEP), Dr. Angela Gardner, president of the organization, had this to say, "Often when you hear that someone has overdosed on drugs you think of illegal substances, such as cocaine or heroin. But parents need to know that many young people are taking prescription drugs from the medicine cabinet. Many of the kids wrongly believe the drugs are not addictive, and they don't realize they can be lethal."

The ACEP survey showed that the types of prescription drugs most commonly abused are painkillers, such as OxyContin and Vicodin, and that central nervous system depressants (or barbiturates), such as Valium and Xanax, are also very common. While boys have a higher overall incidence of drug abuse, this report found that 12 to 14 year-old girls are more likely than boys to have abused prescription drugs, and to have higher rates of dependence.

Anything but a "safe" high

Kids often feel like prescription drugs are somehow safer than street drugs since they come from the neighborhood pharmacy. In fact, these medicines are highly regulated for a reason.

The producers of all of these drugs, such as OxyContin maker Purdue Pharma, maintain that the drugs are safe if prescribed properly and taken only in the recommended doses. The drug companies maintain it is in the altering of the frequency and quantity of ingestion that they become harmful and addictive.

Each type of drug affects each individual in a different way based on a multitude of factors, including body chemistry and weight. Many depress breathing or slow down brain function. Others stimulate the brain, such as amphetamines, and can cause anxiety, paranoia, dangerously high body temperatures, irregular heartbeat or seizures.

Of course teens often will combine the drugs with alcohol, which alters or intensifies the effects further, leading to life threatening situations.

There are a number of steps you can take to avoid prescription drug abuse in your home:

- Keep prescription drugs in a safe, locked place that only you can access.

- Keep inventory of all medications; including prescription and over-the-counter drugs. This includes keeping accurate counts of your pills.
- Stay informed. Ask your doctors, pharmacists and other knowledgeable parties questions about the medications you are prescribed. What are the addictive qualities, the side effects, etc?
- Unused prescription drugs should be returned to the pharmacist. Also, unless the label instructs differently, those drugs can be disposed in the trash.

Abuse of OxyContin is a national epidemic

OxyContin is Oxycodone in a continuous release formulation, made to release its painkilling medication over a 12-hour period. Pills come in sizes of 10 to 80 mg. Unfortunately when abused, the drug is cut up and crushed, then smoked or snorted to deliver that 12-hour dose immediately into the system. You can imagine the intense – and potentially fatal – high that creates.

The drug is intended for relieving chronic conditions such as arthritis and back pain. That led to the first legitimate use in blue collar America. But because it is so highly addictive, by around the year 2000 illegal use was flourishing in Florida, Ohio, Pennsylvania, West Virginia, Kentucky, Maine, and Maryland. In the years since, the drug has made its way across country and "Oxy" is now a nation-wide phenomenon.

It's important to note a very dangerous trend here. Heroin has become one of the fastest growing and easily obtainable illegal drugs in the United States. The stereotype of the old junky shooting up in a dark alley is no longer so. Now it is increasing to kids under the age of 25. For typical stories about this tragic trend, read the article "The damage done: Heroin use soars among local youths, with deadly results" from lohud.com about what's happening in the New York area.

The increase in heroin use begins when teens first experiment, then become hooked on highly-addictive Oxycontin. Oxy typically costs twice as much as heroin. According to a June 2011 report by CNN,

Oxycontin, which costs $6 a pill at retail, fetches $50 to $80 when sold illegally. Since both Oxy and heroin are opiates, and virtually identical chemically, the high is the same. So, as the user's habit increases, they make the switch to the far cheaper heroin.

Oxy, and therefore heroin, can be found in every neighborhood and high school. Don't make the mistake of thinking it won't be in yours. The kids who get hooked on it can as easily be from stable homes in the best suburbs, as from broken homes in disadvantaged areas.

Deaths are climbing from abuse of all prescription drugs, so that overdose from prescription painkillers like Oxycontin and Xanax is now the leading cause of accidental death in 17 states.

The symptoms to look for

Different categories of drugs (stimulants, sedatives, opioids) have different symptoms, but here are some signs that your child may be abusing prescription drugs:

- Sudden changes in mood or personality: does your child get irritable, abusive or negative?
- Defensiveness: when trying to hide a drug dependency, an abuser can become very defensive, paranoid, and secretive, over-reacting to simple requests
- Change in daily habits and appearance
- Memory loss, forgetfulness, or acting clumsy

Also look back to the previous section on Smoked Drugs to learn what physical evidence you can look for at home or in your teen's vehicle.

The next big thing beyond Oxy – Opana

Drug enforcement officials are predicting the painkiller Opana, generically known as oxymorphone, to be the next drug of choice among recreational users. As the name tells you, this drug is simliar to morphine in composition, but is more powerful and twice as strong as OxyContin. Descriptions of the drug say it is prescribed only for moderate to severe pain, which tells you just how potent it is.

The pill form of this medication came to market in 2006, so information is scarce in terms of its abuse. But the drug is prescribed to induce an anesthetic effect, putting the patient to sleep. In fact, an injectable form of the drug, oxymorphone hydrochloride, has been available since 1959, but only as an intravenous drip administered by anesthesiologists in hospitals. So you can imagine the danger, which in medical terms is called "respiratory depression." To you and me that means the lungs and heart stop functioning.

Also formulated as a time-release medication, abusers will be able to slam the full dose into their bodies. The octagonal pills are available in 5 to 40 mg dosages in colors corresponding with the dosage stamped onto the pill. Be on the lookout for Opana.

Chapter 7 - How to Deal with Suspected Drug Use by Your Teen

So now you know what they say and do, and how they think. You also know what to look for so you can recognize the signs of drug use. Now it's time to deal with the problem. There is hope and a way to bring them back. Here we go...

It's a "process"

You may have noticed that "process" is one of the most frequently used words in this book. What are we referring to?

The sequence of events – from your teen beginning to use, to you discovering their use, to dealing with it, to getting the help you need – has to play out over time. Your teen has to progress through several stages – experimentation, accelerated use, rationalization, denial, defiance, to name a few – before they understand they need help and are willing to take action. At the same time, you will also pass through a parallel set of stages – cluelessness, denial, rationalization, learning, acceptance, anger – before you're ready to deal with your teen effectively.

This sequence is what we call the process. While you can shorten its length with effective action, there really are no shortcuts. But at all times you must look ahead to what your next step is going to be. I will say it again, because it's so important: Like a game of chess or checkers, you need to always have a plan for your next move as your teen continues to maneuver against you.

You are going to suffer through a rollercoaster of emotions for months and possibly years to get to where you need to go. It will be one of the most difficult things you'll go through as a parent and family. At the same time you will grow personally, form some of the deepest relationships you've ever had with people you meet along the way, and of course, teach your child some of the most important life lessons they will ever learn.

Get past the guilt

As discussed in **Chapter 5 - The Mind of the Teen Drug User**, there are so many things that go on in our family life that trying to figure out why your child is using is really only a barrier to beginning the work of treatment. You need to eliminate that guilt from the process, know that the drug use is not a result of anything you've done, and move towards how you can make it better.

And this may sound a little strange, but you may need to get angry. Not with anger directed toward your teen, but toward this whole situation that *they* have created. To help with this, maybe you should go back again to the Reality Check chart at the end of the Introduction to this book. Think about how they are conducting themselves compared to your expectations and your standards. Consider how they've dragged you and other family and friends down the slope with them. It's OK to feel the disappointment in them that, quite frankly, they've earned.

This is the path they have chosen. Anger may be the best way to separate yourself from your emotions and natural parental instincts to love and protect your child. It could be the only way that you'll be able to get yourself to take the tough steps necessary to save your teen.

Be a united front

Disagreements between you and your spouse about parental roles or even parenting styles are okay, as long as any differences are discussed and worked out behind closed doors. You must present a united front to your child, for as naïve as they might be in their teenage years, your child will be very perceptive when it comes to getting what they want. Especially for addicts, their whole focus becomes manipulation and to learn who they can take advantage of to get their way. If you don't stand together with your spouse, your teen will quickly figure out what to say to get mom against dad or dad against mom.

I would also never say that one parental approach is wrong versus another. Usually one parent tends to have a certain personality and the other typically has something pretty close to opposite. I don't know if that's a coincidence or a direct relation to roles in the family. Frequently,

I see polar opposites when it comes to parenting styles within most families. I haven't noticed that there are more fathers that are tough or more mothers. Sometimes it's dad: sometimes it's mom.

In certain situations, you'll both need to play a nurturing role, and in certain situations you'll need to be together in "tough love." Just like with counseling, sometimes you have to be more aggressive and sometimes you have to know when to dial it down.

Whatever your parenting styles, the parents I've seen who don't support each other's decisions make this process play out much longer than it needs to. Accelerate the process by getting both parents together and onboard with the program.

How do you deal with others who think they know better than you do?

As the process drags on, you may face the neighbor, aunt, uncle, grandparent, sister or others who insist that they know better how to handle your teen than you. Virtually every time, they won't have the knowledge of addiction and handling teen drug abuse that you have learned firsthand. But that won't stop them from trying to "love" or discipline your teen out of their drug abuse.

Again, communication is the key. Be polite, but firm, and explain the situation and what you are trying to accomplish. Let them know your experiences and feelings, and what you are learning through your support groups and counseling. Invite them to come to your counseling or group sessions.

If that doesn't work, there are no rules when it comes to trying to save your child. If they take your teen into their home, you have to get more aggressive. Don't take no for an answer when you know what's right and believe in what you need to do. Don't give up. Keep calling, or visiting, or arguing – do whatever it takes to convince them they are only enabling your child, and causing them damage, and are not helping the situation. Let them know that you are working with professionals and following their advice through a guided process.

As a last resort, you may want to remind them of the financial and legal ramifications of harboring someone else's child. If you lead with this response, the people taking in your teen are apt to believe it when your child tells them that you are "psycho parents" (you can bet they will).

So at the appropriate step of the process, remind the other adults of the safety issues they could be bringing into their home because of illegal drug use, and the riff-raff that they can expect to start hanging out around their house. Tell them that if your teen hurts himself because of their enabling, you and your lawyer will be knocking at their door.

In summary, I rarely see a good result when a child leaves the home to live with another relative or well-meaning friend, even if they move to another state. You'll just be dealing with an untreated addict in a different location.

At first it may seem better. It's almost like a new relationship. The lasting dynamics of the long relationship with you are removed. The teen will be very guarded and on their best behavior. I'm sure you know that teenagers always are more respectful of others than with you, so you'll hear what a sweet, smart, and wonderful person your teen is. But once they get comfortable in their new surroundings and learn what they can get away with, the child's true colors will surface.

Any exceptions?

Having said that, there is one exception to this advice. Sometimes, when a teen is very advanced in their abuse, going to live with someone else can actually help that teen hit bottom more quickly. If you reach the point where you have to push your teen out of your home, an alternative place to live can provide a relatively "safe" environment for them to fall far enough to realize they need help. Because we know that their drug-abusing behavior won't stop and these well-meaning people will get tired of their act as well. However, I would let this happen only on the advice of a professional.

What if I'm a single parent?

Single parents usually feel like they are navigating this process alone, whether they have a former spouse in the picture or not. For this reason, it is even more important for you get connected right away with other parents for support.

When I first meet a single parent in this situation, I want to make sure that there is no transference of feelings from their own lives. What I mean by that is that they are not struggling with their own issues of being a single parent, because of a lack of a relationship or loneliness. Some parents will be involved in the process in part because of their child, but also in part because of the emotional attention they get from a group. That feeds into their own issues of dependence on the child-parent relationship to define their lives.

For example, a lonely mom may have devoted her past ten years to raising kids by herself. Her lack of emotional support from a partner or spouse affects her decisions. Many times that parent will immerse themselves in their kids' lives, despite a bad situation. Her kids become her relationships, as opposed to healthy relationships with friends or a partner. She's relying on meeting all her emotional needs through her teenage kids. That's not good, and usually leads to poor decisions that enable the abusing teen.

As a result of this situation, Salvador Minuchen identified a concept he called the "enmeshed" family. In this scenario, individual family members have little to no autonomy or personal boundaries. Subconsciously, each family member typically takes on defined roles: victim, hero, etc. As a result, no one is really in touch with their own feelings or preferences. Individuals lose their identity as they are encouraged to mirror the feelings of the family as a unit. Anything that happens to the child, the parent reacts to as if it is happening to them, and vice versa.

This condition in the family leads to adverse emotions and psychological conditions such as shame, depression, anxiety, compulsive behaviors, violence, alcoholism, and addiction. No one is allowed to have individual feelings because that threatens the whole family unit. The person who tries to do something different is pressured to stop and as a result, transfers the family shame to themselves, feeling in some way that they are defective.

This situation can develop with married parents too, but is much more common with the single parent.

The bottom line again for you single parents, is that you must begin to build support through relationships in groups and individuals outside of your family, so you can gain the perspective and emotional strength to help heal the family and tackle your teen's problem.

What if my ex is still in the picture, but isn't helping?

For single moms and dads whose spouses are really not involved, but are very opinionated when it comes to undermining you, you really need to begin by trying to work with them and involve them in the process. As painful as it may be, try to open the lines of communication. Remember it's for the sake of your child.

Also, many ex-spouses who really aren't involved will present like they are. They will make a lot of noise to try to show everyone involved that they are a parent committed to the recovery process, when they really aren't.

I operate from the premise – and would ask you to as well – that no parent wants to sabotage their child intentionally. Many do subconsciously or unintentionally, but no parent wakes up and says, "I want to see my child fail." These parents' actions may seem irrational, but they are just not aware of the proper process.

Make them aware with information. Invite them to counseling or group sessions that you participate in. Tell them the steps you are taking to help your child.

If, after trying to work with them, they are still unwilling to invest themselves in the process, I think the best course of action is to cut them out of it. Your ex is going to do what they want, but you have to do what is right.

With joint custody, you both have the right to make all the key decisions about your child, including school moves, treatment, consequences, etc., but try to sidestep any legal issues the best you can. (Please seek a lawyer's advice on this issue.)

When you start to go ahead with decisions, your ex may object. This is where a qualified counselor can again be an intermediary. Turn the decision making over to the professional. In many situations like this where I am working with the teen, I let this type of passive-aggressive parent know if they have issues with our decisions, they can always call me. They almost never do.

Will psychological counseling help my teen quit using drugs?

Yes and no. When it comes to therapy and recovery, there are a lot of double-edged swords. Counseling can achieve the most benefit when it is part of a complete treatment plan focused on addictive behaviors.

Teen drug users often use psychological analysis and therapy as a way to deflect your efforts to deal with their drug abuse. It can become part of the manipulation game that they play, tugging at your feelings of guilt or concern for their mental health, so they can continue to avoid consequences for their actions.

There have been countless "depressed" or "bi-polar" teens who have come to drug counseling programs, and then have been miraculously cured once they get off drugs. (Which, of course, cause depression and radical emotional highs and lows as very common symptoms.)

Also, before you treat an addictive disorder 100%, the user needs to abstain from drugs and alcohol and get it out of their system. That's not to say that you can't make progress. However, if someone is sincere about trying to get off drugs, it's kind of counter-productive when they continue to use.

Should you believe your child truly needs the help or a psychologist, the most important thing for you to do is find a counselor who specializes in addiction, and preferably addiction in adolescents.

Is alcohol a drug?

Absolutely. Alcohol belongs to the class of drugs called sedative-hypnotics, which includes Valium and Librium. Like those drugs, it is a depressant which slows your brain's ability to think and to make decisions and judgments.

If you're asking this question, step back again and look at the big picture. Unless your son or daughter is 21, they should not be drinking. They don't have the maturity, physically or mentally, to be using alcohol. It could easily get them into situations that could lead to harm for themselves and others, and definitely opens them up to opportunities to experiment with other drugs.

Dealing with drug use for the first time

When you catch your teen the first time, the most important thing for you to do is to educate yourself about what's really going on. You can come up with a plan for consequences, but if you don't have the facts or knowledge you need, that plan is going to be flawed.

You're reading this book, and that's a great first step, but there is also a lot to know about your specific situation. Your kid is learning every day. It's time for you to catch up and keep pace.

Take a moment to fill in some answers and information in the following table. It will get you thinking about aspects of your teen's life that you may be glossing over, and get you researching trends in your community. Ask teachers, counselors, coaches, administrators, law enforcement, or drug counselors in your neighborhood about the questions you can't answer. They will most likely have a handle on trends, who are the "wrong" kids to hang out with, words and phrases, body art, etc. that are common to the drug crowd. The answers here will not be black and white in terms of indicators of drug use by your teen, but the assessment is valuable nonetheless.

Exercise 2: Teen Life Assessment

Question	What you've learned
What type of peers does your teen hang out with?	
What are the websites your teen is visiting?	
What type of music is he/she listening to?	
Any tattoos or other body art? What type? Is it words or symbols? Hair color, piercings?	
How do they dress and what brand of clothes are they choosing?	
What are the current drug trends in the local schools?	
What are the signs and "artifacts" of those specific drugs?	

There are a lot of different variables, but once you've gathered this information, dealing with drug abuse is like dealing with any negative behavior. If you found out your teen was stealing, you'd want to begin setting limits and find ways to restrict them from doing that behavior again. It's the same with drug and alcohol use.

What should I do to stop it?

Here are some appropriate first steps:

- Ground them for a week or two: make sure they understand how strongly you disapprove and that use will not be tolerated while they live in your home
- Restrict them from certain activities they enjoy
- Periodically test your teen, either with home drug test kits or by taking them to a clinic or doctor who can do it
- Talk to the parents of your teen's friends about it

That last bullet item is one of the most important things you can do. Join a support group or build your own "parental prevention squad." Get the names and numbers of the parents or guardians of your teen's friends. Then set up regular calls, or even meetings, to exchange information, rumors, and local knowledge about what your kids are up to, and what's going on in your community.

Twelve-step support groups are also an excellent resource for families of addicts and alcoholics. These groups are structured similarly to Alcoholics Anonymous, in which you work through a number of steps that help you deal with the upset in your life caused by your teen addict. Here are a couple of the most popular:

Al-Anon/Alateen (www.al-anon.alateen.org)

Al-Anon (which includes Alateen for younger members) has been offering strength and hope for over 50 years through weekly meetings and educational materials. Based on the assumption that each alcoholic affects the lives of at least four other people, Al-Anon teaches you about this family disease. The goal is for you to find serenity in the Al-Anon/Alateen fellowship, so that your teen (your "qualifier" in Al-Anon lingo) has less effect on your day-to-day mood and emotional health.

If you go this route, try a few meetings before you settle on one or think this might not be for you. Meetings specializing in parents with drug abusing teens are out there and are more attractive than going to meetings where parents still are dealing with their kids at 40 years old. Many parents find that Al-Anon saves their sanity and their marriages (or other relationships) as they go through this process. Go to the website to find meetings in your area.

CODA (www.coda.org)

Co-Dependents Anonymous is another fellowship of men and women in your situation. According to the group's website, "The only requirement for membership is a desire for healthy and loving relationships. We gather together to support and share with each other in a journey of self-discovery – learning to love the self. Living the program allows each of us to become increasingly honest with ourselves about our personal histories and our own codependent behaviors." Through the support of others going through the same thing, you can discover your co-dependent tendencies, how unhealthy that can be for you and your family and friends, and how to change your behavior to develop healthy relationships.

Smart Recovery

Here's the blurb about this program from their website at www.smartrecovery.org: "SMART Recovery® is the leading self-empowering addiction recovery support group. Our participants learn tools for addiction recovery based on the latest scientific research and participate in a worldwide community which includes free, self-empowering, secular, and science-based, mutual-help support groups."

See **Appendix C - Links and Resources** for more information and places to find support groups.

One group of people that you may have to avoid is those who haven't been through what you are dealing with. When you chose a group of people to reach out to for support, the ones who have experience with teen drug abuse and addiction will provide the best advice. In general, people who haven't walked in your shoes will be several steps behind you, so they'll drag you back to your old emotional states of guilt, shame, doubt, rationalization, and denial. They will stall your progress and cause you to fall back into the old patterns that helped enable your child. There may be a rare person who is so close that they trust you no matter what, but in general you should be getting your support from seasoned warriors in this battle.

The purpose of consequences

Many parents find it very uncomfortable to impose harsh consequences on their teens. They worry that it will drive a wedge between them and their child, damaging what virtually all of us regard as our most precious relationship.

As discussed in other chapters of this book, many parents fall into the trap of listening to their teens a little too much, and believing that their child *has to have a cell phone* or is *entitled* to any number of other material items, freedom, or parental trust. Or you might say to yourself, "Nothing I do is working, so why just make him more angry?"

If you hear that message playing in your head, you are missing the point. Whether or not the consequences work or do or don't anger your child is ultimately not important. The whole purpose in escalating consequences is to create drama. You're stirring the pot so that the teen either listens, or screws up more. You're getting them to see that you are in charge and not them. It does turns into a power struggle, but it's an important one and one that you can't back away from.

Let me expand on a point you may have missed in the last paragraph. Getting them to screw up more is a step forward for you as well. It opens up the playing field. It's not just, "you got caught one time and now we move on." It's "you got caught, you know the rules, you're disrespectful, you're hurting the family, and it's going to stop." The negative response of your teen gives more validity to what you are trying to accomplish as a parent, and makes it more uncomfortable for them as you stand your ground.

You'll also begin to gauge the scale of your teen's problem. A child who's not addicted will generally say, "This isn't worth it. I'm getting in fights, I have to stay home, I lost my car. I just don't want to do this anymore." The budding addict, on the other hand, won't care. You may slow this teen down for a bit, but then they will just defy you once more.

But again, that is a step forward in the process, no matter how it may first appear.

Escalating consequences – repeat offenders

If they repeat their behavior you must begin to increase the level of consequence. Catching them again six months later might be considered normal, but if your teen gets right back to what they were doing the very next week, then they're sending you a message, both of their defiance and lack of control.

At this point, revoking privileges such as a cell phone, playing video games, watching TV, participation in sports, or driving the car are all good leverage to shake up your experimenting teen, or test just how far your addicted teen will go.

More on drug testing

As previously stated, you should begin to periodically test your teen once you catch them using. Your local pharmacy or drug store has drug test kits that you can administer at home. Some also include an envelope to send your sample on to a lab for further verification. If you feel self conscious about buying them at the store, online drug stores are a great way to stock up without having an awkward conversation with a neighbor in the checkout line.

For alcohol, you can buy very inexpensive one-time use breathalyzers. The teen will blow into the tester and crystals in the tube will turn color to indicate a positive test. Something to be aware of is that these tests, being alcohol sensitive, will detect mouthwash use as well. A convenient excuse for your teen, but you'll be able to assess the whole situation to know what's really going on.

Or, if you want to be as accurate as possible, you can buy a meter like police use that will give you a blood-alcohol content reading. Expect to pay $100 or more for these professional testers.

Home tests are only a start, however. Teens can quickly learn to defeat them. They will canvas their friends for clean urine when they know a test is coming, then hide it in their pants or the bathroom. Taking niacin is also a common way to flush THC out of the body prior to a test. Be sure you search the bathroom prior to a test, and even watch them pee in the cup if you want to be sure.

Of course, using a doctor or medical center can also help stop cheating. Some clinics or facilities will let you set up a standing order so whenever you feel the need, you can drop by for a test. Professional tests will give you not only a negative or positive, but a level of drugs in the system so you can see if it is declining or rising. That way your teen can't argue that the positive test is based on last week's use. (THC stays in the body for up to 30 days in habitual users.)

If you are testing, do it randomly, but methodically, so that you don't start letting it slide. Mark dates on your private calendar ahead of time so you both will know it's coming, but won't turn into an accusation each time you do it.

Don't argue

As you know, your drug abusing teen will split hairs and argue the smallest points at every opportunity. You need to stop this cycle by resetting boundaries at home and sticking to them. When you ask your child to do something, expect them to do it. When you open that crack in the door for them to begin a discussion, they will push the door wide open and begin to negotiate everything, and that's when your rules and expectations begin to erode.

At that point, everything becomes a judgment call, injecting emotion and leeway into every decision. That's when you say things that your child will file away to throw back at you later, to show you how "unreasonable" and "mean" you are.

Put a stop to it by simply ending the conversation or walking away. When you don't respond, there's no more chance of ending up in yet another regrettable shouting match with your teen.

The contract

One excellent way to avoid the arguments, is to draw up a behavior contract with your teen. The contract takes the emotion and negotiation out of the equation. It's all there in black and white: each behavior means that a specific consequence is imposed. The contract should include good behaviors too.

See **Appendix B - Contract for Behavior** for an example.

When should you get professional help?

If the same situations keep coming up again and again. If you're having the same conversation with your spouse, or others, about how bad it's getting for months on end, then it might be time to move up to the next level and get some professional help.

Some teens will listen and begin to change. Others will do what you say, but make your life miserable. And then there's the kid who'll flat out walk out the door, telling you, "You can't ground me. I don't know what you're thinking. See ya."

The frequency of drug use and bad behavior is very important in the process. You need to monitor both closely because they will help you know when you need more serious help, and probably counseling.

I think parents usually know in their gut what they should do, but they are very uncomfortable about doing it. Common fears are that friends or co-workers will find out, that you have to admit that yours is not the perfect family, or feelings of inadequacy from not being able to deal with the problem on your own.

You probably are also second guessing yourself on whether your teen really has a drug problem or not. Now is not the time to worry about making that call. If you over-react, then the worse that can happen is that they get some good drug education and they understand how strongly you are against use of drugs and alcohol. On the other hand, if you don't move now, and they are developing the cravings and habits that lead to addiction, the consequences can be dire.

Judge your teen by their behavior as well. The steps we'll describe in the next few sections deal with much more than merely getting your teen "sober." Consequences and counseling deal with behavior, as much or maybe more, than the drug use itself.

Remember too, that at first, it's not an all or nothing proposition. Counseling can begin at a low level and move up from there. Think of the professional as your partner in dealing with this problem.

Give yourself a break and let a professional become the bad guy for a while. Remove you and your emotions from the equation by letting a counselor set the expectations and deal out the consequences. Getting you off this hook for a while can really relieve a lot of the stress from your family and be a start to dealing more effectively with the problem.

As we've discussed before, you need to get past your emotional reactions and on to getting help for your child. One thing I hear all the time is, "We probably should have brought our kid in a year ago."

What does professional help consist of?

There are a number of levels available, from outpatient, group counseling, to more intensive outpatient programs that include individual counseling, to residential programs where patients stay at a facility 24 hours a day. Hopefully you're working with a qualified drug counselor at this point who can guide you to the proper form of care.

See **Chapter 8 - The Elements of a Good Program** for more detail on professional counseling.

The life or death importance of standing your ground when drug use escalates

In the face of months and years of fighting your teen, many of you will find yourselves reluctant to push your child harder and harder with escalating consequences and revoking of privileges. It is natural for you to feel that way, but if your teen has a problem that's not getting better, you need to overcome your natural, protective instinct.

I almost hate to even qualify that last statement with "has a problem" because that is an out that many parents will take. They will continue to deny to themselves that their teen is involved in anything more than recreational use or experimentation. They won't be able to overcome the thought that they can fix the problem themselves.

If your teen's behavior is progressing, prepare yourself now to begin to detach your emotional self from the process of getting your teen back on the track to a successful and happy life. For those kids who can't get a handle on their drug or alcohol use, the ultimate outcomes are either jail or death.

And no, that's not an overstatement of the problem. When your counselor and your support group tell you that your child is an addict, you need to step back and see this situation for what it is, and do whatever is necessary to get the help your teen needs.

When you read the parents' stories later in this book, you will see that most had to make extremely hard decisions to save their child's life. Many had to force their teenage child out of their homes before the process could play out. On the streets, your teen will finally face a reality that they can't see at home, where they are enabled by you to artificially survive and continue their behavior.

Law enforcement and legal implications

Local law enforcement can be another tool for you to use when your teen is out of control and will not listen to you. Call the local police or sheriff on these offenses:

- When your underage child (under 18) leaves the house without your permission, call the police and report them as a runaway. Local police will take a description and take them into custody if they find them. The result, at least for the first few times, is that they will just return them to your home.
- If your teen is skipping school – even if they won't leave the house in the morning – it is your responsibility. If they refuse to go or you get a call that they are missing during the day, report them as truant.
- If they ever threaten you physically, even if they seem like they are bluffing. When you tell law enforcement you feel threatened, they will respond.
- Your teen enters your home without your permission, especially if they are 18 or over.

- They are in possession of stolen property.
- Causing damage to your home or contents, such as punching holes in walls or breaking windows, appliances, or electronics.

Continue to report your child for these types of incidents, even if law enforcement doesn't respond the first few times. They will start to log your calls and complaints and build a file on your teen. They will begin to know your son or daughter. And they will get tired of dealing with the calls. A stint in juvenile or adult jail will most likely follow.

This is another thing in this book that may seem counterintuitive at first, but legal troubles resulting in jail and/or probation can be a good thing. It could be just the jolt your child needs to get his or her act together. We're talking short term stays here – one or two weeks maximum – not long-term incarceration which can actually drive people deeper into the drug culture.

If they put themselves in a situation where they are caught with drugs, are selling, or facing a DUI, don't shield them from those troubles by bringing in the lawyers or pleading with the judge. A few nights in "juvy" and follow-up probation can be a humbling experience. You might think it would even "scare them straight" and in some instances it will. But unbelievably, the kids who are still in denial or have developing addictions will soon forget the experience and go right back to what they were doing.

Once your teen has been arrested, they will usually be assigned home supervision and a probation officer (PO). Here are typical terms of a first offense:

- They are either at school or at home, nowhere else
- No friends may visit and no associating with old drug buddies
- Must stay within eyesight of you
- Must wear an ankle bracelet tracking device at all times
- Of course, no alcohol or drug use, subject to periodic testing as proof

Now you've got your teen right where you want them! Any deviation from what the court orders, and your next move is to call the PO. Cut and dry, black and white. They   behave or they are back in juvy or jail. You've taken a major step in regaining control of your home.

Still need more convincing this can be a positive step? Let's look at the potential liability your teen can cause you. Who will pay when your drug or alcohol influenced teen causes bodily injury or property damage? It could be in a car, or it could be just an act of violence or vandalism while under the influence. Of course it's you who'll pay the bill. Are you ready to risk college funds, savings, investments, your house – your very lifestyle – so that your teen can keep a "clean" record?

So ask yourself, what kind of "relationship" are you maintaining by protecting your teen at home? Is it based on the values that you want in your house? Is it a relationship based on mutual honesty, trust, respect, and love? No? Then stand up to your teen's behavior.

How do I get to that point?

This is where support groups can be very positive. There, you can listen to and learn from the stories of those who've walked in your shoes. This is an attitude that takes time to develop. It's against all of your parenting instincts to withdraw your support. I can tell you to get tough, but hearing it from parents who've reached that point, and how they got there – that's what will get through to you.

Blame and guilt don't matter. You need to try new things. To listen to new ideas. To recognize that collectively, the group wisdom will teach you the right thing to do. Turning your child to the streets and the harsh reality of the real world may seem unthinkable at first, but it is a fear you need to overcome to finally regain the child that you've probably already lost.

Convincing your teen that there is life – and fun – beyond drugs

Many times in group, teens express the feeling that they don't believe there is any way to have fun besides partying with drugs and alcohol. They say everyone does it. Which you would believe too if you listened to pop music, spent time on the Internet, played countless hours of video games, and watched an endless stream of television that glorifies the party circuit, getting wasted, and hooking up. The emphasis on shallow pursuits such as looking cool and being popular, and getting the right "stuff" is pervasive.

That pursuit starts at younger and younger ages too. Teens coming to my groups regularly pronounce that they are "almost 15" as a five year-old would say "I'm not five, I'm five and a-half." And they say it as if they expect me to reply, "Oh well, you're all grown up then. Go ahead and ignore your parents and do whatever you think is best."

You may have tried to limit the type of TV shows and websites they can look at, but it isn't easy is it? You can't always tell which is the good stuff and which is the bad. Plus, they have other ways to access it outside your home.

The quick (yet artificial) mastery of music, flying a jet plane, fighting, or playing team sports offered by video games creates a feeling for lots of teens that life should be the same way.

This is a cultural problem, yes, but one that this generation of parents has also brought on itself. A key error for many parents is in making children too much the center of the family. Today's parents have over-reacted to the emotionally-distant parenting they received with parenting characterized by the "helicopter parent" stereotype. They just can't do enough to keep their kids happy, which, when it comes to drug treatment, leads to huge issues of entitlement that are almost as big a problem as the drug issues. Keep that in mind if you have younger kids.

However, as the vast majority of us know, there is a huge world out there with pursuits that are very enjoyable and fun without drugs and alcohol:

- Building real relationships based on integrity and caring
- Studying and mastering a discipline that takes long-term dedication, such as a new language, music, martial arts, or sports
- Community involvement with charitable organizations or a church
- Internships in a profession of interest
- All-ages concerts
- Spectator sports
- Extreme or action sports   to get a good adrenaline rush

100

- Just plain hanging out and playing cards or board games, and watching (good) television or movies
- Sober parties organized by sober young people's groups
- Video games, as long as there are limits

As the earlier generation of parents used to say, only boring people get bored. Kids just need to refocus and regain perspective to realize that "lame" activities are really not that at all, but just a label coming from a self-centered attitude. They need to get outside their own little world and get some experience in real life.

As you can read in **Chapter 10 - Stories From Those in Recovery**, experiencing life on its own terms, with all its ups and downs, is what leads to far greater satisfaction and happiness than any artificial substance or pursuit of material things.

I will say that this is an extremely difficult concept for a young, immature, adolescent brain to grasp. When your teen truly becomes a young adult at 18 or 19, they'll be in a much better position to listen and understand, but don't you think it's worth a try?

Chapter 8 - The Elements of an Effective Program

If you have advanced to this chapter, you know your teen's abuse can't be fixed without professional help. As discussed before in **Chapter 7 - How to Deal with Suspected Drug Use by Your Teen**, there are a number of levels of programs to help your child:

- Support and abuse education groups that you attend one or more nights a week are typically the first step. You can find them through your teen's school, through professional drug counselors, or though organizations such as Alcoholics Anonymous (AA), churches, and teen centers.

- Detox programs get drug users who are at more advanced stages of addiction past the physical addictions of drugs such as meth amphetamine, OxyContin, and heroin. These programs, lasting from days to a few weeks, should be supervised by medical professionals. These programs simply rid the patient of the drugs, but must be followed by a good recovery program to change physical and mental health for the long-term.

- Individual counseling sessions once or twice a week. Again, we recommend a specialist in drug counseling, not a generalist. The benefit here can be limited by the short amount of time devoted to the program each week, compared to a more intensive, multiple-days-per-week program. Individual sessions can work for people who are highly motivated and wanting help, but usually aren't as effective for a resistant teenager. Think about how long your teen has been building their habit. Can you overcome those years of built up cravings and behaviors with an hour a week?

- The Intensive Outpatient Program (IOP) is a step up, comprising several meetings a week with an individual counselor, over a period of six weeks or more. Often AA meetings are included as part of the IOP. Your counselor will usually periodically drug test your teen as well.

- In-patient or day programs. These are several-days-a-week education and therapy sessions that are another step up in intensity. A typical program might be five days a week for eight hours a day.
- Residential care is the final step when all else fails. There are many levels of residential care, from lockdown facilities that contain teens, to sober living housing where residents are free to come and go. Boarding schools, wilderness camps, and long-term recovery programs are all available. Duration can be as little as 30 days, but better programs will extend for at least 90 days and for as long as one to two years.

Alcoholics Anonymous (AA), rather than Narcotics Anonymous, is usually where counselors direct drug abusers to attend meetings during recovery. Why? First, alcoholism and drug abuse or addiction include most of the same behaviors, so the recovery path for both has much in common as well. Also, most recovery programs will use the AA "12 Steps." As you learn more about this topic, you'll see that the 12 Steps are more about rebuilding one's life, living with integrity, overcoming destructive behaviors, and building healthy habits than about simply getting clean and sober. "Working the program" to address personal character defects is more important than just getting clean.

Group counseling

Group counseling is a good first step into the world of professional drug counseling. Usually you'll want to take this step when your teen continues to use, even after you've caught them and laid down consequences to get them to stop. These groups are about dealing with bad behavior – defiance, lying, manipulation, laziness – as they are about stopping your teen's drug use.

You can find counseling groups through your teen's school, through professional drug counseling companies, churches, Boys and Girls Clubs, and teen centers. Or ask friends who've been through the process of helping their teenager or other family member who they would recommend.

There are many types of groups, but the one I run is once a week. We cooperate with a local school district, which refers kids whose drug use is catching up with them in the form of failing grades, suspensions, expulsions, or legal trouble. Professional drug counselors run the group, along with student services personnel who are usually the first people to deal with kids in trouble.

Our group is a mix of parents at all stages in the process of recovery. That provides a range of experience and input to everyone attending. Some of my parents have been coming for years, and their input is invaluable to new parents, like you.

During group meetings, you and your teen will eventually be expected to share your story. It's a little un-nerving at first, but you need to be open and honest in telling the group what's going on for the leaders to provide effective help.

Remind your teen that these are people who have heard every story (and lie) there is to tell. Your child can either waste the group's time with the story they want you to believe or they can tell the truth. If the group hears, "I've only done pot. I only did it a few times. It's been a month since I got loaded," you can bet that the heat will get turned up to reveal the real truth. Make it easy on yourselves by being honest up front.

As families continue to come to group, we periodically check in with them and monitor their progress as we provide advice on dealing with their problems. You'll often learn things to help your own situation from hearing the stories from other parents. And soon enough, you'll find that you can begin sharing your experience to help families new to the group.

This "circle of life" in group counseling is one of the best aspects of it. Beyond the help for your child, the process will begin to heal you and your family as you escape the hold of a household that revolves around a teen drug abuser.

Gather phone numbers and emails from parents who you think have common stories to yours or who you feel comfortable talking with, but are farther down the road and have experience you can draw on. Then call those other parents for support between meetings.

Additional things you should know about group meetings

Effective group counseling usually takes a very direct approach, so be prepared for a dose of reality when you first attend. Drug counselors genuinely like most of the kids they work with. They make it clear that their sole purpose is to help. But when we speak to them, we will challenge them in a number of ways:

- As mentioned before, you should never believe the first story any kid tells and you can expect group leaders to bore in on them to get the truth
- Disrespectful conduct towards anyone else in the group is not tolerated and they should be asked to stop or leave the group
- Teens need to participate and work with the counselor – taking up a seat is preventing someone else from getting help who really wants it
- We need to stir them up because that's what initiates action and change, so we don't care if they like us or not (most don't, at least at first)

A warm and fuzzy, comfortable approach is usually not what teens need. In fact, if any group you attend conducts its business that way, it should raise a red flag. No disrespect to parents, but most teens probably have been treated with kid gloves for too long at home. The initial approach has to be tilted more toward shaking things up. Then, once the teen is less resistant and more ready to make changes, you can shift to a more loving approach and deal with the underlying feelings.

When you go to a group with your teen, keep your comments to a minimum. Push your child to talk and don't tell their story for them. So many times, parents come seeking help, then proceed to dominate the conversation with justifications of what their teen is doing. Often this is an ego thing for parents who want to demonstrate that their kid "isn't that bad" and that they are good parents and on top of the problem. You will defeat the purpose of the group if you talk too much.

Remember that you don't need to defend yourself or how you've parented your child. Again, that's a natural instinct for you and a perfectly understandable initial reaction. But now is not the time to put up with the stream of BS that most of these kids pour forth to their parents and think they can get away with. No one will attack you as a parent or what you've done in the past, unless you keep coming to group and don't make the changes you need to.

Those other parents who may seem so wise now? They were just like you only weeks or months before. Nearly every parent in the group has experienced and done the exact same things that you have. So let your guard down and don't try to protect yourself or your child. The group is the place to let your teen expose what they're doing so they feel the full impact of it on their lives.

Intensive outpatient programs

The most common next step after group meetings is the intensive outpatient program, or IOP. We move to this level when the teen needs to change their thought process. The goal of IOP is retraining your teen on the issues at hand when they are still resistant and challenging what we teach in group meetings.

At this point we want to ramp up the intensity a notch and impose more structure on the teen to focus them more on learning a new way of thinking. Though there are many varieties of this program, usually lasting for six to 12 weeks, here are some of the elements of my 12-week IOP:

- Three days a week and three hours a day for a total of nine hours each week
- Four to six teens in each IOP class
- Each three-hour session will usually include one hour of education on the physical and mental affects of drugs, an hour of individual counseling, and an hour where we work with the group together
- Introduction of alternative coping skills, how the disease affects the family, and relapse prevention
- Individual research and writing "homework"
- Phone support to you and the patient during the week

- Three other meetings during the week, usually 12-step AA meetings aimed at young people
- Finding an AA sponsor within 30 days
- Periodic drug tests to ensure your teen is staying clean
- Monthly follow-ups for six months after the end of the program to monitor and evaluate the teen's progress and sobriety
- Community service

As you can see from the preceding list, this is indeed an intensive program. Combined with school obligations, extra-curricular activities, and maybe even a job, your teen will be very busy. Of course, by the time they are ready for IOP, they probably aren't spending time with friends, so this fills the time when they would be sitting at home wondering what to do. It works out for everyone.

What is the success rate of these programs?

People ask me about success rates of treatment, but I always try to shy away from numbers on that one.

Go into the program with goals in mind. I will work with a parent and say, we want to get your kid off drugs, out of legal problems, doing better in school, not running away, and lowering their high-risk activity. If we can be successful on three or four of those, and cut out the drug use, most parents will be very happy.

So look at it more in terms of minimizing the damage than complete success or failure, and compare it to what was going on. If you've got a teen who's now finishing high school, taking care of legal problems, not stealing; you've turned around a lot of the behaviors that were leading them to the problems they faced just weeks ago.

In-patient programs

Psychiatric hospitals are the home-base for in-patient programs. The length of these used to be 30 days and then the person would be returned to their old life. You can imagine that the success rate was not that great. Next time you hear about the celebrity-of-the-month getting "clean" in thirty days, take that with a huge grain of salt. That simply is not enough time.

As a result, in-patient programs are usually just a detox and jump start for a longer recovery program these days. Their main objective is to stabilize major problem areas for the patient. Then a good program will recommend further treatment at either an out-patient or residential facility.

Residential care or boarding schools

When all else fails, or when the teen is a serious danger to themselves or you, this is the ultimate option. A good program is going to be at least a year.

The goal of the program is to get the addict clean, modify the behaviors that have led them down the wrong path, and get them back on the track to a productive life. For older teens, residential care will set them up to live independently on their own when they finish.

For the younger teen, boarding programs, wilderness camps, or schools for troubled teens are the right choice. Most of these programs are facilities that keep your child contained in their physical facility. Many are located in very rural or wilderness areas where there really is no "escape."

All residential and boarding school facilities should incorporate a family element as well. Family meetings and counseling are necessary to heal and educate you, after you've been worn down by living in the small, intense environment that an addict's behavior creates. As your teen gets better, you need to be reminded that they still have the disease, and that things will deteriorate once again if they return to the old environment. The family counseling part of these programs helps immensely in that regard.

To find a good facility, rely once again on the drug counselor who's led you this far. And of course, the personal network you've begun to build as you get help for your teen will be a great resource here as well. See **Appendix C – Links and Resources** for a listing of some facilities and links to other directories.

Why does residential work?

By the time your teen is recommended to a residential program, you will have exhausted many options trying to get them to change. At this point, it's almost certain that they are an addict. As with any disease, you need the best help you can find, just as you would with any other medical condition of this magnitude.

Just like diabetes, cancer, or a broken leg, this is something you can't fix at home. The same goes for the disease of alcoholism or addiction. There is no mending this with remedies from your medicine chest. You need to get your teen into intensive care.

Also, at this stage, the family unit is usually extremely broken. The tension, mistrust and resentment between you and your child block any meaningful communication. It's best if you both break away from this dysfunctional situation.

Peer pressure – positive peer pressure for a change – is a key element of good programs. A group of men or women, going through treatment together, can build tremendous bonds, and will be able to influence each other in ways that you or a professional counselor never can. Another young person who's been down the same road has an edge in credibility with your teen. Your child will be able to see themselves in that person, and see the rewards of a sober life. Those people won't let your teen continue their pattern of lies and manipulation, because they've lied and manipulated in the same way.

Again – that's a game that has been played before, and your child's peers in the recovery house or sober living facility will call them on whatever BS they try. They will insist that your child get honest with themselves, to really dig into their destructive behavior, learn the character defects that led them to drugs, and learn how to begin living with integrity and humility for the first time.

Your teen will have expectations set for them again. Just as you tried to structure your home, they will wake, eat, and go to bed at reasonable times, they will have chores and other duties to maintain a clean house and functioning family unit. And they will either comply or they will no longer be welcome. (Don't be surprised when, after a few weeks in residential recovery, you teen suddenly has "learned" all kinds of basic life skills that you spent 15 years trying to pound into their heads. Just be happy and know you laid the foundation for that.)

Your teen will be free to try a new way of life, without feeling like they are "wrong" and you are "right." They can get a little of the independence that we all seek and start to expand outside the small box they've created for themselves at home.

And guess what else? You will sleep well again for the first time in years, free of having to police your child, and knowing they are safe and doing the right things. The sight of your teen, bright-eyed again and growing into the person you always hoped they would be, will transform your well-being too. If you had any doubts about the price of the program, trust us, the serenity you begin to feel will be worth every penny!

How do I find a good program?

A lot of times people will see a counselor and assume that counselor is qualified or know what they are doing. That's a bad assumption. Before your teen sees a professional for the first time, sit down with the counselor and be very direct and ask questions:

- Are they a specialist in **teen** drug and alcohol addiction?
- What is their experience and education in the field?
- What methods and programs have they seen that are effective?
- Do they have references and success stories?
- What is your treatment plan for my child?

A counselor's job is to create change, whether it's positive change or negative change. You need to know what I'm going to do to get that done. Very few parents ever call me out and ask me why? How is this going to help? Parents need to put more accountability onto the counselor.

I will stress again that you need to see a specialist! Counseling has a bad reputation in a lot of ways, especially when it comes to chemical dependency.

One sample of a list of questions you might ask is from Father Martin's Ashley Treatment Center. See that list of recommended questions here:

www.fathermartinsashley.com/ABOUT-ASHLEY/faqs.aspx?id=50

Qualifications you should look for

To research drug counseling certifications in your state, you can go to this online directory of addiction study programs maintained by the Addiction Technology Transfer Center (ATTC) and funded by the Center for Substance Abuse Treatment (CSAT): http://nattc.org/dasp/main.asp. This directory lists the study programs, but you can use it to find the resulting certifications you should look for.

For example, in California the CADC designation – Certified Alcohol and Drug Counselor, granted by the California Certification Board for Alcohol and Drug Counselors – is a good one to look for. Professionals who are CADCs complete the following course of study:

- Three-year program (community college programs are often every bit as good as a 4-year degree)
- Intensive courses in chemical dependency, and the science behind alcohol and drugs
- An internship requiring 6,000 hours of on-site training at treatment facilities

The internship part of counselor training is probably more than necessary, but when it's done, that counselor will have a good sense of their skill level and the confidence to work with almost anyone. That's where the best counselors get the growth that helps them learn and do it right.

Will insurance pay for treatment?

This is a case by case answer. It depends on your insurance company and on the condition of your teen. When insurance does pay, they will require pre-authorization and then will usually cover just a few sessions at a time before they want an update from your counselor and another pre-authorization to continue.

However, you may want to think twice before you make an insurance claim for a drug recovery program. Once you do, it will forever be on your child's medical history. That will cause problems later when they apply for regular health insurance. You should consult an insurance professional (not with your provider) on this matter, but an individual who's been through drug rehab is not a good risk for an insurer.

If there is any way you can afford it, I recommend you pay cash and keep it off your child's medical record.

Can you afford it?

In answer to this question, a corresponding question has been asked of parents many times in my groups, and each time it seems to have the desired impact; "If your child had cancer or another lethal disease, would you do whatever it took to find the right treatment to make them well?"

The disease of alcoholism is no different. Whether death comes quickly though an overdose, car accident, or run-in with the wrong people, or whether it is a long, slow death by years of abuse, addiction is a life or death situation. When your teen has advanced to the stage where you need professional help, you need to somehow find a way to get them the treatment they need.

There's another way to look at it too. What will it cost if you don't pay for treatment? These figures are a little dated, but still show that there are definitely costs for not pursuing treatment. The Brandeis University Schneider Institute for Health Policy calculated these results in their 2001 study titled "Substance Abuse: The Nation's Number One Health Problem:"

- $400 billion per year in untreated addiction costs in the U.S.
- At $133.2 billion per year, untreated addiction is six times more expensive than heart disease (America's number one killer), six times more expensive than diabetes ($130 billion annually), and four times more costly than cancer ($96.1 billion per year)

Here are some costs that might hit your pocketbook if you don't take action:

- Wrecked cars
- Damage to the home
- Legal fees, fines, and court costs
- Lawsuits when your teen causes harm to people or property
- Increased insurance premiums
- Extra school expenses for repeated classes or catch-up work
- Added years of dependence on you for room and board.

Finally, this cost won't impact your finances directly, but as we've said before, the likely alternative for addicts not seeking help is jail or prison. According to "The Economist" (June 2010) the average annual costs of keeping an inmate in jail ranges from $18,000 in Mississippi to approximately $50,000 in California. And we guarantee the environment will be a whole lot less hospitable in lockup than in a recovery home.

Chapter 9 - Stories From Parents Like You

To preserve the anonymity of those involved, the initials you see here are not the actual initials of these individuals and were chosen at random based on an aspect of their story.

AL and CL – Son

AL(dad) and CL(mom) tell the story of their teen who turned from a bright young boy to an out of control, angry alcoholic who had to leave their house, live on the streets, and sleep in a dumpster. Once they learned about the disease and took action, their son finally found his path to a new life.

AL: He went to a small Christian school for most of his life.

CL: He wasn't studious. School was OK, but it was just something fun to do that gave him friends. That's what school was all about.

AL: He had a real good relationship with his older sister. She was three when he was born. When our son got to the age where he was talking, she would play school with him. She actually taught him his ABCs and how to read.

The relationship with his middle sister was different. She kept more to herself. But it was generally all good.

CL: Just regular brother and sister stuff. They all went to the same school. The girls were there and he went too. Because of his sisters, the teachers all adored him. Until a few years later.

He started to have issues with a few of his teachers. He would get up and wander when he felt things were boring in class. But no learning disabilities or anything like that. He was very social.

AL: Our son never would come home and start in on his homework. You had to get him to do it. But once he did, he did well. He'd rather be doing something else. His grades were average to above average. It was in grade school when he had discipline problems begin.

But you've heard the expression, "Don't do the crime, unless you're ready to do the time." Well he was one of those who was very willing to do the time. He was willing to take the consequences, but still keep doing what he wanted to.

CL: He really was doing fine until ninth grade. He had met some kids around the neighborhood. He was still in the little Christian school and no one else in the neighborhood went there. He was into BMX bicycling. I think that's when he started.

AL: We started getting phone calls and he started getting detentions. The school was located at the church, and when we would go to church we would see a lot of the teachers. They would tell us things that our son was doing. So we didn't have formal sit-down meetings, but it was coming to the surface.

CL: It was the summer between his freshman and sophomore years when he was at home. He and his friends started smoking pot. He told us later he bought it from a guy in the parking lot at a fast food joint.

Caught for the first time

CL: The first time he got caught we got called from the school because he was smoking pot on campus. That was the first clue I had that there was any problem. I really was clueless. I burst into tears. It had never come up with our daughters, so this was our first exposure to this kind of problem.

We had talked to the kids, you know, "Hugs not drugs." We told them this is not something we allow in our home.

AL: I told them stories of classmates I had in school who had gone off the deep end and ended up homeless.

CL: There was a guy in the neighborhood that we know. His nickname was Rabbit. Right before our son starting doing all this, he had been arrested and that was his third strike, so he had just gone to federal prison. Rabbit had come home to live in a tent in his parents backyard because they wouldn't let him live in the house. He was on parole and he was all tatted [tattooed] up, and he had talked to our son.

AL: He told our son, this is what it does to you. It seemed to make an impression on him, but only for a while.

CL: They called us into the school and told us that our son had been caught on campus smoking pot. I just went to pieces. I thought, oh my God I can't believe this. They told us they were going to expel him and all I could think was, that's going to look terrible on his record. So they said, you can pull him out of school and then it won't go on his record as an expulsion. It was in April and so close to the end of the year, that we home schooled him to finish 10th grade.

We sat him down and said, we won't allow this, so you *will* stop. And he said yes, I will. So we thought, okay, we're done with this.

AL: He was with us virtually 24 hours/day then, because he would go to work with me. He would do his classwork after that. He stayed in a motor home on our property.

CL: Right at this same time he had an older friend who had already graduated. The friend's grandmother had kicked him out of her home. I felt sorry for him. Our daughters were out of the house, so I thought, "Maybe this boy just needs to be exposed to a good home." (Laughs) So I did it and even allowed him to use our car! Of course it turned out he was using too, so we finally put our foot down and told him he had to leave because we found a beer can in his room…which actually turned out to be our son's.

CL: We didn't do anything else to him after he got caught. He was in public school by then and there was no support or help at all.

We figured we just needed to go to church more and be on top of him. But that didn't work, obviously. During the summer we had his friends over because we figured they know that we don't allow it. In fact I allowed them to dig up my whole yard and build berms and jumps for their BMX bikes, thinking that they'll be busy and won't get into trouble. So that's what they did all summer, was build the BMX tracks in my yard. And get high.

His friends seemed OK

AL: It was the typical thing where we thought they were okay. They looked nice like him. They weren't the dregs of society. I would even take them to work and they would ride in the area around there. On the weekends I would take them places to ride too. At that point in time I didn't see anything that led me to believe he was into it, but he just hid it very well.

CL: He really never was disrespectful up until right before he got caught. It was when his dad wasn't around and because I would allow it. I was just trying to keep the peace and keep him happy.

He never cursed, but he would scream and yell a lot. He never damaged the house. He was respectful in a certain way. Other than one time when I got so angry that he was smoking pot in the back yard, I was pounding my fists on his chest. He pushed me away, but I just landed on a bed so I wasn't hurt.

AL: When I was around he would go up to his room or never say anything.

He and his mom were in an argument. I was doing the dishes and had a dish towel in my hands. When he wouldn't stop, I threw the dish towel at him. He took one step toward me, but then he stopped. I tried to egg him on, figuring we could have it out and move on. But he didn't bite. From then on he just avoided me. We would pass in the house and not even look at or acknowledge each other.

CL: So he was never physically abusive.

AL: In fact, we would get into these shouting matches, and every once in a while he would have a moment of clarity. And he would say, "I really don't want to do this." I think it would finally click in his head that he was starting to lose control, but it wouldn't last long. Of course now we know that he was powerless over it.

From pot to narcotics

CL: It wasn't until the end of his junior year and into the summer that he got really bad. He started using cocaine. We were drug testing him for the marijuana and it kept coming up positive, but he would tell us that the drug test was no good, that it was a bad test. We believed him!

Just before the end of the summer before his senior year, I told him I was taking him to the doctor. I had been told that now is the time to do something because he's only 17, and wouldn't be 18 until February. So I was scrambling to do something because I could tell things were getting out of hand.

I finally told him I was going to take him to the doctor to be tested. He kept throwing it at me that he was going to take off if I made him do it. And of course, I was scared to death that he would take off.

I finally took him to the doctor and he gave her the OK to give me the results and the doctor said, yes, he is positive for marijuana. At that time the cocaine didn't show.

I thought if I could get him into a psychologist, that would fix him. So through my insurance we found a therapist. She had told him that she would keep everything just between the two of them, and only relay something if she felt he was in danger.

So school starts and he got suspended pretty soon after. He goes in and talks to the therapist, then I go in and she starts to tell me everything that he just said. He came unglued because she broke his confidence, and he got up and walked out.

My husband didn't like the therapist either. So from then on, I didn't know what to do.

Just get him to graduate

AL: So the plan then became to just get him through high school.

He went through three suspensions from the new public school, which all took place from late August to March of the following year. If we could not get him through high school. At this point I just felt like, when he walks across the stage and takes his diploma, he can just keep on walking because I didn't want him around anymore.

C: He turned 18 in February and he kept threatening to take off. I had found out through a friend of his who was going to outpatient counseling, about that group. I kept telling our son we should try it. But he would always say you make me go and I'm going to leave. And at that stage, I kept thinking, oh my God, I have to keep everything okay and under wraps.

In April, he got suspended for the last time, and we said this is it. We finally took some real action. We started taking things away from him.

We even took the door off his room.

Then one night he had left the house and we didn't know it. He had set his alarm to wake him up to sneak out, but he had forgot that he set it. I was in the living room and heard the alarm go off about 11:15. When I went to check his room, he was gone. We waited up for him to come back. The next day he left home. He said, "I'm 18 and I don't need this."

At 18, he left home

AL: He left our house in April the day before Easter and was gone for six months.

CL: His grades were so bad, he was failing his classes, so we had him in night school just to get enough credits to graduate. But when he left home, he dropped out of school.

AL: We were talking to the counselors at school, but we weren't getting any help there.

They had nothing in the way of assistance. They referred us to one local facility, but they said since he's over 18, he would have to call them. They couldn't talk to us.

The problem affects the family

CL: It caused a lot of tension in our marriage. I would hide things that our son was doing so that AL wouldn't know about them. My whole thing was trying to keep their relationship good, which actually was a mess anyway. And trying to keep him in school and help with his grades.

The worse it got, after he left home, AL just shut down. He didn't want to discuss it.

AL: I took it very personally, that he left while I wasn't home. That to me was the final nail in the coffin of our relationship. I thought of him as basically dead.

CL: It was like we just shouldn't talk about him. If he doesn't want to be here, then let him go.

AL: I saw what it was doing to my wife. I would try to communicate with her, but she was keeping things from me, so the frustration set in and I would just say, "What's the use?" I didn't do anything after that. It was just going to run its course. I was done.

CL: When he left, I started going to a Thursday night group counseling with another couple. It gave me a lot of information and a lot of strength. I learned it wasn't something I could fix, which was a 180 from my thinking before. We weren't the only ones with this problem. I had been so embarrassed, especially at our little church. The shame, the embarrassment and the guilt that I couldn't fix it. That's what I based all of my decisions on.

But really I needed to base them on the facts. That our son had a problem and we needed to get him help. So going to those meetings was opening my eyes.

AL: Before that, I'm frustrated because she doesn't want us to talk about the problem with other people. This stuff was building up in me, but I didn't feel I could talk about it with anyone else, because of the shame she felt. And we didn't talk together either.

CL: Finally he began calling and leaving messages on our answering machine when he knew we weren't home. The first time was on Father's Day, which just pissed me off. Then he called to get his birth certificate so he could get his driver's license. We had never let him get it before because of his behavior.

AL: Of course, unbeknownst to us, he was driving anyway. We hung the keys up by the door, so when we weren't home, he'd grab them and take one of our cars.

The family begins to get help

CL: Then in August he called me at work to ask if I could talk to his dad and let him come home. I told him he had messed things up, and he needed to call his dad himself to make it right.

Of course, the only reason he wanted to come home was because he was getting kicked out of another house and didn't have anywhere to go.

But by then, I had been to the groups, and I was beginning to see that he needed a program. We were getting stronger.

AL: As she went to the meetings, I got to the point where I started asking about it. She started talking about it and we starting formulating a plan in the event he did want help.

During one of those Thursday meetings, she met the kids from a residential recovery house in Los Angeles. Afterwards, she was walking three feet off the ground because those guys looked so good.

CL: I said if he ever comes home, I know where he can go!

AL: We started doing research and formulating our plan, to say okay, if he does call, we know what we're going to do. His leaving the way he did was the best thing that ever happened to us because it left us alone to start communicating and think about what we would do next. She really took it by the horns and started the process.

CL: The first time he came home was in September. He was doing pot, cocaine, and crystal meth. He weighed 105 pounds. Shoes and pants duct taped together. Later on, after a few weeks in residential, he told me he "thought I looked pretty good. I had cleaned myself up." He looked like death.

AL: He was stealing from us. While he was gone, he was getting into the house and taking stuff. Until I wrote him a letter that said the next time you get into our house, we're calling the police and will have you arrested.

CL: We told him he needed to be in a program and complete it, or he couldn't stay at home. Through my insurance we got him into an Intensive Outpatient Program at first. From that, they recommended him to a 30-day in-patient program. Well, he talked himself out of that within a week. Then he went to an intensive day-hospital program, but got kicked out of that within days because he was still using and had a dirty drug test.

You can't come home unless you get help

AL: That was the last straw. I went to the place and picked him up and then dropped him off at [a major intersection] near our house. I told him, if you can get a plan and want to do something, then come by this evening and we'll talk about it.

He came to the house that night and told us he knew he needed to do something. I told him to call the insurance and see what kind of programs are available, and he did it. He told me they referred him to another inpatient program at a hospital. I asked him what he was going to do. He called and they told him to come down the next day for an assessment.

CL: We packed up his stuff and we dropped him off down there. But he called about 5 pm that night and said, "I'm not supposed to be here."

Well, we said no, that's okay, you just stay there. But it turned out it was a dual-diagnosis [clinical psychiatric diagnosis] program, so he actually wasn't supposed to be there.

AL: I got a call the next day from the director who told me that they were not going to be able to help him. What he needs is long-term residential treatment. We told her we knew that, but were just working through the process.

So I dropped him off at the same intersection again, and said if you have a plan, come on by. Sure enough he shows up.

CL: He asked for the name of the drug counselor. So I gave him the number and he called and made an appointment for that Saturday for an evaluation.

AL: After the evaluation, the Thursday night counselor gave us the number of the residential program and said go up there and take a look at it. He told us that he needed to go up there, that we just needed to give him the chance to fail.

We did go there for a visit that next Saturday. After seeing the residential facility, we thought, this is the place he needs.

And sure enough, that same day, our son was supposed to go to treatment, but he didn't make it. He said he couldn't get there on the bus, but by that time we told him he either needed to stay in treatment or he was headed to residential. There was no tolerance.

CL: He hadn't gotten himself to treatment and he had stolen more money from us. So at that point we told him he needed to go to residential or pack his bags and leave. He said he would go, but still he said he was going to go visit his friends before he left.

He called a friend, but the friend didn't show, so he ended up just walking down the street with his bags.

He kept looking at me like I was going to jump up and tell him, "Don't go. Don't go."

AL: This was Tuesday, but he called the next day and said he made a mistake and would come home the following day and go to residential. I had made plans to go out of town, so I left on Thursday and she was by herself.

Into residential treatment

CL: I told him we were going up on Saturday. I packed the car and headed north.

When we got there, we sat through their usual Saturday family meeting (all residents and their parents). It was an 18 month program, but we told him it was initially a 30-day commitment.

The director told him to think about it for the next couple of days, and if this is what he wanted, come back on Monday morning.

And I was like, "Oh nooo!" I've got his stuff in the trunk. Please take him now!

Sure enough, the whole way home he was angry and telling me I had lied to him about how long the program was. I told him I hadn't lied, that he could commit for three months and then he was on his own if he didn't want to stay.

He wanted to go to his friend's place when we got home and I dropped him off. I told him he better be back on Monday morning, or just don't come home. We had it arranged to change all the locks to keep him out. We told all the neighbors that if he [didn't go to residential and] showed up in the neighborhood, we would call the police. And we made sure he knew that too. He had no alternative.

An hour later, he calls to get picked up. He was still working on me, telling me he was going to get $400 from a friend. I told him, that's fine. After we got home, he said he was going to go to his friend's again. I told him, do whatever you want, just be here Monday.

An hour later he was on the phone again, wanting to come home and go to residential. He found out his friends were all done with him. They kicked him out too.

The next day we took him to residential treatment.

AL: He stayed there, but really wasn't working the program. He was still lying to us. He wasn't doing his step work like he said. He was just marking time. He had a bed to sleep in and three meals a day, and that there was no option at home.

I was like a lot of dads; I had never lied to him. I was agonizing over that as the three months got closer. I figured I needed to keep that promise. But I never had told him that if he did three months and did OK, he could come home. My out was that I had told him he needed to complete the program.

But someone asked us, "How many times has he lied to you?" We may have lied, if you want to call it that, but it was to save his life.

But it was a moot point anyway. He didn't want to leave after the three months. But he still really wasn't all about the program, so at 10 months they "grouped" him. The director told him he couldn't just stay there, he either needed to work the program or leave. They had his clothes in a bag on the front porch.

CL: At that point he knew he couldn't leave. He knew that the type of person he was, he would die. The program taught him about himself. When he used, he used until he was completely wasted. He couldn't leave any drug or alcohol left over. He knew if he used again, he would take it to the max again and be dead.

Epilogue

From that point on, he took to the program full force. He earned privileges. He finished adult education and got his high school diploma. He finally earned his driver's license. He worked at several different jobs. And he graduated the program in 2005.

While still in one of his other jobs, he started working as a part time manager at the house. And a year and a half later, the program director asked him to become a full time manager at the house.

It still was not clear sailing for AL and CL's son, he's been through a lot since then. He lost the job as house manager, and endured financial problems and hardship as a result. But through all the ups and downs of

his life, he now has the tools and support system to cope . As of the
writing of this, he had six years sober and had been rehired as a house
manager at the same residential treatment facility.

AL: "We've stayed involved with the house (treatment facility). I will help them in any way I can because of what they gave me. This whole experience has been amazing. To see him now – I can never repay that."

AM – Son

AM's son started out with a few cards stacked against him, but still found drugs and alcohol was nothing more than a destructive, temporary fix. AM's home was a typical household in a nice home in an upper middle class neighborhood – two parents and three kids.

My son was challenging. We found out that he had learning disabilities when he was in second grade. He really didn't do so well in school, starting back in pre-school. With him being the oldest of my kids, I had nothing to compare to. I didn't know if the people giving me this information were the experts, but it turned out they were right.

He went into a private kindergarten because they didn't think he could handle public school. Education-wise they could see the slowness and how difficult it was for him.

When he was diagnosed with learning disabilities, it still wasn't clear what specifically was wrong until middle school. Then we found out it was severe dyslexia.

When we look at why he became an alcoholic, I was told there sometimes is a traumatic event. They realize the substance makes those feelings of inadequacy or low self-esteem go away. I think in his case it was the feelings of inadequacy because his reading and writing skills were so far below normal. He was ridiculed. He was taken out of class all the time for special education.

He also has told me that as a high schooler, because of his size and being so tall, when he would go to parties he could drink more than anyone else. That earned him some "street cred."

He was sixteen (high school sophomore) when it started for him. He started coming home drunk. Then at 17, he went on a trip to Europe with the high school. I didn't know this before they left, but they were going to let them all into the bars there because they were all over 16, which is the legal drinking age in many countries.

He would call home severely drunk. Then the stories started coming to us afterwards and we think he was literally drunk during the whole trip. His souvenirs of the trip were all alcohol related: a flask, shot glasses, absinthe. I found them in his closet. He went through all his money like crazy. I think that was the single event that launched him into alcoholism, and he would agree.

Sometimes I think back and wish I hadn't sent him on that trip. I was very angry at the school for not having more control over the kids. But then again, looking back, God seems to have a reason for everything that happens. If he had this experience when he was away at college or outside our home, we would not have been able to get him help. He could have died. The amount he was drinking, he probably would have died from alcohol poisoning.

The way we first dealt with the problem was a lot of yelling, screaming, begging, pleading, bribing, threatening. We took things away. We had his car all the time. I had a special place where I would park it away from our home. If he knew that I had the keys, he probably would have beaten me up to get them. So I made sure he couldn't find the car; that no one could find the car. I really had to hide it deep into the neighborhood.

Those consequences never worked.

Learning the right way to deal with the problem

Just about this time we were introduced to our first drug counseling group. My son was 18 and a senior in high school. At first it was one meeting per week.

Thankfully, because all of this chaos was going on, I had been seeing therapists, psychiatrists; I was trying to figure out what was wrong. First I was trying to find out if this was normal for an 18 year-old. I'd get a call from the vice principal at school complaining about his attendance record, so I asked if his behavior was considered normal or not normal. She said this is very "not normal" for an 18 year-old and he has the worst attendance in the school. That was one trigger.

Then I went to a psychiatrist. I read a laundry list of all the things going on, and I asked him also, is this normal. He said absolutely no. And he told us we needed to kick him out of the house and let him sleep on the streets.

So that was my first introduction to tough love. Was I prepared for that message? No.

He always struggled and had a lot of trouble with his grades. With six weeks to go in his senior year, he was in danger of failing five of his six classes. We decided then that we weren't going to invite anyone to come for graduation. No family or friends.

He actually did pull it (graduation) out, because he manipulated the heck out of every teacher. He was belligerent, and a bully. To his teachers he was disrespectful, and then would be respectful in the next moment. We got constant calls, but I didn't know what to do.

One night he came home really, really drunk. He drank vodka, so we could never smell it on his breath. But he was getting more and more out of control. Eighteen, driving, and drunk. The therapist told us we needed some help for him.

By the time we hit on this drug counseling group, it was like, "Oh, finally someone who understands this." One of the therapists referred us to the group. That was the beginning of the road back for us.

Our counselor did the normal intake. When we first went to group, we were amazed to see friends there; the last place we would have expected that. In that environment, with a lot of other teens, he did not hold back. He began to tell his story. Instead of downplaying everything, he told it with more detail and accuracy.

After he did that, the others in the group started in on him. I finally started realizing how very serious it was. So we started doing whatever the counselor said.

But it didn't take long for him to blow it. That's when we started the intensive outpatient program (IOP). He was good for about two weeks, but soon went back to his own thinking and got drunk again.

I found alcohol in the car and the counselor told me that he needed to start an IOP today. But my son said no, and if I made him go, then he would kill himself.

I called the counselor and told him what he said. As we were on the phone he started to tell me exactly what to say. Then I put him on with my son. "Now that your mom has hired me, I can see that you are a threat to yourself. I'll call the police, they will assess you, and put you away for 72 hours for observation."

Then the counselor asked my son if he wanted that. Of course he said no. So the counselor told him, "Get your a** to treatment today." And he did.

The next step: outpatient treatment

When we got to the program they asked him (for my benefit) were you going to kill yourself, or was that just a threat to get your mom to stop dealing with you. And he admitted it was just a threat. So that's something you learn, most of those are idle threats. You just deal with at least the first one seriously, and they'll back down.

So, as parents, we start learning that you can push to that level without giving in to your fear. I started getting more comfortable with what the counselor asked me to do, but not always.

I was just as disobedient as my son got sometimes because I was pushed out of my comfort zone. I remember one time my son had called his counselor late at night, ranting and raving that he hadn't got some privilege back from us. The counselor told me to take his cell phone away, but I wouldn't do it. I was using the cell phone as a way to be sure he was still alive. I hadn't got to the point where I could let go and let the process take place.

What I do today when I help others in the same situation, is to try to give them the courage to do some of those things that I couldn't do. I didn't have any other parents to help me through that.

My husband was out of town all the time. He worked across the country and it didn't make sense for him to always come home. It was just me. As a result, the resentment that built between my son and I got very extreme because there was no one else trying to make him stop. My son also hated the counselor, because I let him tell me what to do and followed his advice.

For my husband, he always supported me because I'm very analytical. I never do anything spontaneously. While he supported it, he didn't understand it. He didn't get that my son was an alcoholic. He didn't see all the daily behavior that I saw.

I didn't have the help that others have, but I didn't have time to think about it. As long as I had my husband's support and he wasn't in conflict with me, then it was OK.

Moving on to residential treatment

So my son began the outpatient program, but within four weeks, the counselor said this isn't going to work and he needs to go to residential treatment. Just about this time I had some friends going through the same thing and they came to the same conclusion. The other father and I took a trip up to visit a recovery house in April. The next week, their son was admitted.

For me, it took another five months for me to get there. I decided after I visited that he wasn't as sick as the guys in the recovery home. He wasn't doing heroin, he was "only" a binge drinker.

But the counselor was patient and we continued treatment. My son broke all the rules and had tons of consequences imposed, but the counselor hung in there and waited for me. Then the summer after he graduated high school, everything fell apart. I could see at that point that my son had become a danger to us and our home. I couldn't ignore it anymore.

He was a monster. He developed so much power in the household that there wasn't a single thing that I would tell him that he would do. He would fight me on everything. Not physically, but he would pound on tables and cuss to levels I'd never heard before. He stole from us. He was constantly leaving whenever he wanted to.

He was 18 at that point, so we really didn't have to keep him in the house. It was just me keeping him there. And then the counselor could see how dangerous it was. I was home alone with him, so he insisted that my son go.

I went to see the counselor with my husband and I saw something in my husband I've never seen before, which was, "I'll do whatever it takes to protect my wife." So to know that he's going to do that, and to put his son out on the street, I was surprised actually. I thought he would say, "You can figure this out."

Damage to the family

Now I also had a very enabling family, so I had to call all of them and tell them not to take my son in. Brothers and sisters and mom and dad. They all thought I was crazy.

I knew they would impede the progress of getting help for my son, so I invited them all to come to the residential home. Almost all of them were there with me when we went to see it. Only one of my sisters didn't come, and it was actually that sister who was causing a lot of the problems. And it was just about that time that my husband's mother was dying, so again, he was not available.

My son was at his absolute worst then. He did not care how he affected anyone. I could cry, I could scream. He didn't care. His sister, at the age of thirteen, was scared. He didn't care.

Our younger son shared a room with him. When the screaming matches happened, there was our other son trying to sleep through it.

The younger one became addicted to video games as an escape. World of Warcraft in particular. Severely addicted. As soon as we kicked my son out, we got a therapist to work with the younger one. It took us about 3-4 months. The addiction to video gaming is very real. The transformation I saw in him was shocking. He was exhibiting the same behaviors as a drug addict or alcoholic, but he didn't have the substance. It was so sad to see.

And little sister was also trying to sort it all out as a 13 year-old. We still have the damage. Our daughter really loves her brother. She has anxiety issues because our house was so unsafe. And I got blamed for that because I couldn't control my son. She is in therapy and my other son refuses it, but he really needs it. He has no respect for his older brother at all, even though his brother is now years into sobriety.

Into residential, but not ready to surrender

Right before he finally went away to residential treatment, the drug counselor and I had a conversation, and again I expressed my doubts and asked if he was sure my son needed to go. He said, of all the kids he'd seen in the past year, my son needed to go more than any of them. He told me, with his binge drinking he's going to die. Other people who smoke pot or drink some every day, they'll last awhile. But my son is going to die. I finally said OK.

His last request before he went was to ask for a $20,000 loan and he could take care of everything and get his life in order. This is how delusional he was. And we told him no, of course, and not only that, we don't want to see you until you agree to go to the recovery home. We made sure to tell him that aunts, uncles, neighbors, grandparents – no one wants to hear from you.

As we unveiled all these consequences, it finally hit him and he started breaking down and crying. He finally said that he would go, but that I was not allowed to drive him there. He still wanted to punish me.

I said, "If you think this is a war between us. You going to residential treatment is *not* me winning. If you feel like you won, that your ego needs it, that I'm a terrible mom, whatever. Just get in the car and go."

To get him there we had to orchestrate everything. They promised me that if I could get him there, they would make him stay. The plan was that we would leave him at the facility. He had been a few days sober when he got there. Fortunately they took my son's ego and turned him around right away, and he committed to stay.

At first, it didn't go well at all. He was an a**hole and they didn't like him at all. After six weeks he ran away. I got the call in the middle of the night from the manager.

He stole all the money he could find and took everything he had and went out on the streets. That's how naïve they are. He didn't know that in this direction was a dangerous neighborhood and that way was somewhere else bad so he ended up in [a heavily gang-ruled and high-crime area]. All kinds of things happened to him there, but he eventually got a bus ticket back home.

We didn't hear from him for two days. I called every single friend I could think of where he might land and told them please don't take him in. None of them did except for one. She took him, but told him he had two days to make a decision.

By then he was ready to go back, and the house managers told him OK, but told me not to bring him back there. Because my son's ego was so big and he was so arrogant, they had to break him. So he had to find his own way back to the house.

The second time in, he still struggled. There were signs that he wasn't doing well. At about nine months the manager called and told me that it was not working. That they didn't know what to do with him. They didn't want to give up, but it wasn't working.

I knew that some of the boys were seeing a psychologist [who specializes in addiction] from our area. I suggested that my son should see him too, so they set it up. That's when things finally started to shift for him. He had been there about 11 months, but that's when he finally surrendered and admitted that he had a problem, which is what it takes.

Finally, recovery takes hold

That's also when he got his dual diagnosis. He was diagnosed as a narcissist in addition to his alcoholism. It was interesting because he said the psychologist would figure out what was going on. After about three sessions my son called all excited. He said, "Mom, mom, I know what's wrong with me." I said, oh you do? And he said, "They said I'm a narcissist."

He was very relieved to know that. He refers to his dual diagnosis to explain why he does what he does. I think it allows him to figure out how not to behave like that anymore. I think it helps him understand himself. I know people hate to label people, but in this case, the label makes him feel like he's not going crazy, and that there's hope.

But he still had to be clean and sober first. And the environment of the recovery home forced him to work on it, so he didn't use it as an excuse. He learned how to cope with it without the alcohol.

He was feeling better about everything and stopped going to the psychologist for about six months, but things really started to go badly again. So we've got him back seeing him again for support.

The work doesn't end with the finish of residential treatment

Now my son is a graduate of the program, but that doesn't mean the problems stop.

His first group of roommates didn't work out – one got drunk and the other had ego issues.

He started doing some really crazy behaviors. Staying up until five in the morning. He decided to spend $1K on plants, but didn't have money for that. Bought a carport, but didn't have money for that. He was buying furniture, but didn't have money for that either! He got banned from interacting with other people from the facility. He was out of control.

When he started coming to us for rent, I wasn't sure what was going on. We hadn't seen his house that much. With the job market the way it was at the time, we were helping him out along the way with some money. Then I started visiting the house.

I was like, "Where did this stuff come from?" I started realizing that my "rent" money was paying for the fun stuff. He wasn't taking responsibility, so we cut back.

He started getting let go from his jobs then too. Pretty much from every job he's had. So it's all caught up with him. We just bailed him out because he had attorneys threatening to seize assets. Which, I'm not sure what they would seize because he had nothing. He was under threat of being jailed because of his court fees. His wages were being garnished because he went to a Payday Advance and never paid them back. He was at the bottom financially.

He had credit cards and spent that money. He had a TV that was $1,000 and was not paying off his bills. He couldn't find jobs because of the economy, and he refused to work for minimum wage because he thinks he's better than that.

The residential facility managers gave him a business plan to hang Christmas lights with his roommate and that fell through as well. Then they wanted to wash windows and clean rain gutters. Unless it was a regular paying job, I didn't want to help him with these whimsical things. It takes two years to start a business, and he doesn't have the money for that.

Financially he was a mess. He got really depressed. It was hard to watch. He always put on a good face for us, and has stayed connected to the recovery house. I would ask the managers and they would tell me he was going to be OK.

My philosophy was that, as long as he stays connected to the house, he's going to be OK. Even if he was homeless, they will give him a bed to sleep in. Or if he was hungry, they would give him food.

My own "program"

Prior to my son going to residential treatment, our friends and I were doing two meetings a week. We went to the group drug counseling meetings and their son needed to go to another meeting, which we would all go to. I was ranting and raving at one of the meetings, and this other parent there said, "You have got to go to Al-Anon."

I didn't know what it was, but I took that suggestion and went for a while. When my son went into the recovery home I said, I probably don't need those meetings anymore. Everything is under control now.

Then he ran away from the recovery house.

So then I figured I needed it more than ever. Since then, focusing on myself, and the disease of alcoholism, has made my life a lot easier. The goal is serenity, no matter what the alcoholic [qualifier] is doing. And I have a lot more peace. Especially in the past year with all that's gone on since he graduated.

I go to the recovery house and go to Al-Anon meetings, and go to our counselor's group meetings too; each a couple of times a month. For me I have to be constantly reminded of the power of the disease. I keep on thinking it's going to go away. And I want to keep blaming myself.

I did all the right things. I was a very involved mother and had the kids in activities all the time. We had a nice home and provided a very nice life for our kids. But even all that didn't keep my son out of trouble.

By going to Al-Anon I don't blame myself anymore, and by talking to others, I can see it is a very active disease. It is constantly present.

My husband tried Al-Anon, but it wasn't his thing. He lets things go, but I don't. I don't consider myself damaged, but I obsess about people, places, and things. I recognize that now and I try not to make some of the silly decisions I did before.

The lessons I've learned

Sobriety first.

I saw such a tough year for my son after he graduated the program, yet I saw a young man choosing sobriety despite everything. He had to sell his car to pay rent. He lost jobs over and over again. He had to ride a bus for six months to get to a job. He has really gone through a lot. But we told him he needed to stay connected to the house, or we would not support him. Fortunately he has taken that very seriously.

He finally found his niche as a car salesman. He works for an Acura dealer and is doing a wonderful job – one of their top salesmen.

Was that the purpose of this year? Maybe it was. That he learned that sobriety is more important than anything else. I definitely learned that he can make it through anything. I just hope that one day he'll look back and see all that he's accomplished.

Also, as a parent I got distracted by his learning disabilities. I got distracted with his dual diagnosis, and with his depression and that he might be suicidal. I was always in fear that if I didn't help him, that he would drink again, and that it would be my fault because I didn't help him. That is wrong thinking.

From the time we started with our first drug counseling to admitting him to residential treatment was seven months. If I had connected with other parents sooner, I might not have wasted the five months that I did, and put my other two kids through what they went through. I would have had someone to move me along.

I had so much fear. My son manipulated me by telling me that I was just making all my decisions based on what our counselor said. He told me that the counselor was no good.

The counselor really didn't have any track record that I knew about. He could have just been someone off the street. Of course, my son played into my doubt all the time. And unfortunately, it worked for those five months.

My logical side said this totally makes sense. I see him working with many kids. I see many of the kids in recovery. All of that fit together. But the boy that I love was telling me I was making a horrible mistake. I was constantly going back and forth in my mind.

That's why today I spend so much time with parents going through this process. I tell them to call me. Not everyone does. Only a few have the courage to go down the right path. Especially when they have to kick their child out of the house.

As a parent those are the feelings we're always fighting. Fortunately, through the group meetings at the recovery house, Al-Anon, and with listening for two years, I've learned that I cannot force him to drink. It's the basic "Three C's" that Al-Anon teaches: I didn't cause it, I can't control it, and I can't cure it.

I'm not buying him the liquor and I'm not pouring it down his throat. This ultimately is all his decision and his choice.

BB - Son

Even after getting their son into residential treatment, this family lost him again to drugs. BB is a classic case of the dual personality of addicts. They can be productive and models of living the program, but they can just as easily swing 180 degrees and be the worst of addicts. With BB now in jail, his struggle with addiction is on hold. But there are many lessons still to be learned from his story, even without 100% success.

He was a great kid. A lot of fun to be around with a great personality. Charming. Athletic. Very smart academically.

There were some behavior issues in fifth grade with his teachers. We didn't really see anything that I was too concerned about until sophomore summer. I just thought it was adolescence and not anything major.

The problem was, he would speak his mind and teachers did not like that. Sometimes he spoke his mind in situations where he shouldn't. We tried to teach him that sometimes you just have to keep your mouth shut. But I kept getting calls from teachers. It was disruption, speaking out, wanting to give the answers because he thought he knew everything. That kind of thing.

Still, his freshman year in high school was great. Good grades and playing lacrosse.

The summer before his sophomore year, he was 16 and a-half. We went ahead and let him get his driver's license. By that time he was already using, but we didn't know.

This baffles me, but he said he started in third grade. I didn't believe it. In third grade he was never out of my sight. When could he be using in third, fourth, fifth grade?

But it *was* possible because his best friend lived about five houses away, in a cul-de-sac. He told me later on that the older sister of this guy got them high for the first time when he was in third grade.

The reason I didn't notice is that he would spend the night up there and that's when they would do it. It was not very often. Maybe once every four or five months, something like that.

I think in middle school it became more frequent. At that point I thought he was fine, so I was giving him more freedom. He could ride his bike to school and go to the movies with friends. I'm sure it started happening more at that point. I think it was just pot at that time.

I'm not sure, but I think in his freshman year he started using pills (prescription meds). Sophomore summer is when it started getting out of control.

Immediate action when he's caught for the first time

I'll never forget it. He walked into the house and my husband and I were sitting on the couch. It wasn't late, just after work, maybe 7:00 or 7:30 pm. And he walked in and said "hi" to us, but walked straight back to his room. There was just something wrong. It was gut instinct. My husband and I turned to each other and he said, "He's high."

I went to his room, but there were no signs. His eyes weren't bloodshot, but something was off. So that night I went out and searched his car and I found a bag of pot. Of course we heard the usual answer from him: It wasn't his, it was a friend's. I didn't believe him.

Within that week, I downloaded Guardian® Monitor onto our computer [tracks all computer activity]. It was awesome. Devastating, but awesome. I could read his chats and get on his [social networks].

What came up was shocking really. I had to get on Urban Dictionary to find out what most of the stuff they were talking about was because I had no clue.

After seeing that, I just knew that my son was a liar. He is insecure and he tries to build himself up to others by telling stories. So I thought maybe some is true and some is not, and it may not be as bad as it looks.

I was in denial. You don't want to believe it. "Not my kid..."

I used to talk to him all the time about drugs because it was rampant in my family. My stepdad died from it. The thing was, I would always talk to him about street drugs, never about prescription drugs. I'm glad to see it's getting more news coverage now. I had no idea about that. I was telling him, "Don't do crystal meth like your cousin."

Even in a program, careful monitoring must continue

So we took him to visit a drug rehab program. We talked to them, but decided against it. Then we went to another recovery program. He didn't complete that. We pulled him out. They were buying and selling drugs on their breaks during meetings, which we found out after we pulled him out.

The reason we pulled him was that I got on the computer and found out he was trying to sell pills to everyone. I called them and they said bring him in and we'll confront him with this. Our son said he was lying; that he was just trying to look cool. And they said that kids do sometimes do that. Since we had no proof, we had to give him the benefit of the doubt. I left there feeling really uncomfortable, and thinking, "Are you kidding me?"

That night at 2:00 am my husband heard something and he went to his room and when he opened the door he was sitting there with pot, bagging it up for sale. We took it and called the cops. My initial reaction was right, but then I got scared.

So we pulled him out of the program after we found him with the pot. That was not working for us.

We had lost control of him. He had gone to Mexico and got caught trying to bring back Zanex. Sneaking out. Things like that. We took everything we could away from him. He had nothing; even the door on his room was gone. His cell phone. I stripped his room of everything. Took the computer and hid parts of it so he couldn't use it.

One thing about him, no matter when I called or how high he was, he always answered his phone. I never really understood that. If it was me, I wouldn't answer. I'd think, I'm in trouble already, I'll just have fun right now. But he would always answer. I'd call three or four times in a row and tell him he needed to get his a** home.

He'd tell me no. Later he told me he always answered because he didn't want me to worry. Are you kidding? With everything going on you don't think I'm worried? But in his head he thought he was doing me a favor.

Though you may feel helpless, keep pushing

I called his friends' parents so that we could all work to get control of them together. That didn't work very well. Some parents aren't very receptive. In fact, his best friend – I later learned – his parents were hiding stuff from us. They knew a lot of things before I knew. But they figured it was OK as long as they [he and the friend] did it in their house so they knew they were "safe." You know, boys will be boys.

Unfortunately their son is a heroin addict now.

I really didn't know what to do. I was on the computer and on the phone constantly calling people. I felt lost. I didn't know where to go next or what to do. We would tell him he couldn't go out, but he would just look at me and say, "You can't stop me."

It was not long after that he left the program. Within a two week period of time right after he was out, he got arrested at school for possession with intent to sell. They sent him home and he was supposed to stay there. We had to go to work. As soon as we were out the door, he was out too.

Three days later I got a call from the police that they had him and he was high. They asked me to pick him up at the police station and I went and got him. Then five or six days later he took off for two days and we couldn't find him. He had gotten totally wasted, stole a friend's truck, and crashed into a fire hydrant, continued on and hit some trees, and trashed the truck.

I got a call from the cops and they were bringing him home. I said, "Are you kidding? What's it going to take? Is he going to have to kill someone for you guys to take him to jail?" Very frustrating.

We had called the police on him five or six times. Three days before, we had asked them to please take him to juvenile hall. They kept telling us to wait for his court date. It got to the point on one of the last times we called, they came to the house and handcuffed him and lectured him, but our son just laughed at them. He knew at that point that nothing was going to happen. They didn't do anything so many times when he was caught, that he was just ignoring them.

I told them my husband's not home and I don't feel safe. It had gotten to the point where he was scaring me. When we figured out what was going on and tried to regain control and get him to stop, that was when he got very angry. He had punched holes in the walls of our house. I told them they can bring him to my house, but I'm not letting him in.

We kicked him out, but it didn't really matter, because he went and lived with my mom. But at the time, I couldn't honestly say I could kick him out on the street. It was easier for me because I knew he had somewhere to go. I had that pretty easy.

They finally took him to juvenile hall. He spent about 30 days there. Getting him in there was probably one of the best things that happened because he got under the judge's thumb. He was on probation for one year and they laid out a plan of what they wanted him to do.

That's when we first went to a drug counselor and our son started an intensive outpatient program. Things were just OK. He was still not doing some of the things he was supposed to do.

Listen to your gut

I have a bad tendency to dismiss my gut feeling. Through the whole thing it was saying, "Something's not right. Something's not right." But he seemed like he was doing OK, so I thought, I'll just see what happens.

He was supposed to graduate the IOP program, but he didn't – and he shouldn't have. It was the last day of his IOP, after it was already extended, and he tested dirty. We found out he was using Oxycontin. He was smoking Oxy. He hid it. They know how to do it.

The counselor told us it was time to go away to a residential treatment house.

It was a Thursday that we told him he was going, but we didn't take him to the recovery house until Saturday. I thought he was going to run. We had a group meeting that night and he showed up. I was surprised. The counselor told him at the meeting that if he shows up to go, then he would know he was ready, but if he ran, that he should keep running because he had nowhere else to go.

143

I left for work on Friday and my son was sitting in a laundry basket full of clean clothes in the garage just sobbing. I was thinking he was going to run. There was nothing I could do, but just go to work.

He did take off Friday night for a couple of hours. He went and got high one more time on Ecstasy. Then we took him up to the house on Saturday morning.

[He was prepped for a long time; for weeks. He was told that this is what he should do. By the time it was time to do it, he was ready to go. A lot of kids hear "residential" and run away. But he heard it for so many weeks that he was convinced this was the best thing to do.]

Into residential

He was just there for the first few months, but I finally started to breath. Of course, as soon as I took a breath, he ran. He left the treatment house after about four months.

He took a cab to the train station and took a train back home. He ended up downtown, then took a cab straight to our house. He said he would go anywhere else, he just didn't want to go back there. He said he was frustrated.

We told him that's the only choice you've got. I told him, you don't have to go back up there, but if you don't, I have to turn you in to your probation officer and they'll put you back in jail. By that time he had been court-ordered to finish the program. So those were his two choices.

He said he wanted to call the recovery house manager, and he did. They talked, but they wanted my son to find his own way back to the house, just the way he found a way to get home. He wasn't home for even 24 hours.

[Again, he's the classic drug addict. When he is sober and working the program, he is a bright upstanding citizen. When he's using drugs, he is pedal-to-the-metal, full blown, nothing is off limits.]

That's his personality. No matter what he does, it's 100 percent full force. When he was playing lacrosse, practice started at 5:00 pm, he wanted to be there at 3:30. He didn't care if no one else was there. He would run…Everything is tunnel vision with him. That one thing is all that matters.

And when he was at the recovery house, that's how he was with the program. He got really into it. He had been expelled from high school, but he graduated up there. He wanted to go to school; he wanted to be a drug and alcohol counselor.

Unable, and unwilling, to deal with less structure

But once he graduated and moved out, he just didn't transition well. He moved out and started struggling about a month after that.

One of the other graduates – the day my son graduated – told me that he would have a really hard time when he moved out. He said that my son was so involved in the house, that he was going to struggle outside of that structure. I talked to the managers, but they thought, "This graduate doesn't know what he's talking about."

He knew. It didn't take long.

My son was making comments to me, but I didn't really see what they meant. In my head I thought he was doing really great. He would say things like, "I feel like an old man. All I do is work and go to meetings." He said he was bored. There was nothing to do. Now in retrospect – I can see he was having a hard time.

I didn't ignore the comments. I tried to direct him back to the program, but I didn't see it as the big problem that it was. I would tell him to go ask the program managers what he should do. And he would, and they would give him a hundred ideas on different things that he could do, but he wouldn't take action. It didn't take him long to just spiral down.

Part of it was that he hooked up with an old girl friend. That was pulling him back home. She was going to a university north of where he was living. They were together about a month and a-half, then she broke up with him.

At that point, he lost it. I've never heard him like that. He was so emotional and so distraught. I actually thought he was suicidal.

He was already having such a hard time. His counselors said here is what you're doing that you should change and asked him what he was going to do about it. And he answered that he didn't know. Well, he knew. He knew what to do and what the answers were from the program.

No excuses. He could have gone back into the program and made it right, but he didn't. He had that opportunity. I don't know why he didn't. We had it set up. All he had to do is make a call and they would bring him back into the program and go over what he was dealing with and how to move forward. He made the call, but then within an hour he called them back and said he wasn't going to do it.

I was devastated. That was a really hard time for me…very emotional. I thought for sure he was going to go back to treatment.

Back to the neighborhood, with predictable results

Even when he decided to move back here, we told him he couldn't live with us. I called everyone in my family and told them, "Do not let him live with you." If he calls, tell him to stay and work it out with the recovery house. He was already in touch with people back here at home. It was sucking him back in.

But his best friend and his parents moved him back and let him live with them. They kicked him out two weeks later. I confronted them on that. They thought that our son could help them with their son. I told them it doesn't work like that. The only thing that would happen is that our son was going to get dragged back into the drugs.

That's exactly what happened. As soon as my son started using again, they kicked him out. He moved in with some girl.

When he got here, he was working for a little while, but he didn't look good. He lost his job. He quickly became very sick. He was sleeping at a drug dealer's house and someone stole his car. What did he expect? He called us and wanted us to give him savings bonds that we were holding for him so he could buy a new car. He called the police on us when we wouldn't give them to him. That's how delusional he was.

He was using Oxy at that point and he didn't look good. He was really skinny and drawn. It was really scary. There's that part of you that knows what you need to do. But part of you says, if he walks out that door and doesn't make it through the night, am I going to be able to live with that guilt? I know what you're supposed to do, but sometimes it's not real easy.

My mom let him live with her again too, though we asked her not to. She would say things like, "I keep buying whipped cream, but when I go to use it there's no gas in it." And I'd say, "Mom, it's him. Kick him out." [He was huffing the propellant.] But she just couldn't do it.

He was just staying there, but wasn't doing anything – good or bad. He was just there. He was doing work around her house to earn money to pay off a traffic ticket. She gave him the money to pay the ticket and he disappeared for two days.

He didn't pay the ticket. He bought $200 worth of Ecstasy and Xanax, and whatever else he could get his hands on.

Another big mistake

We didn't know when he moved down here that he had bought a BB gun. He kept it under the front seat of his car like some kind of freakin' gangster. The whole mentality. He got high with a couple of his friends and went into a convenience store. I don't think the other two knew about it [the gun]. It was impulsive and I think it boils down to my son wanting to look cool.

He pulled out the gun and set it on the counter and said, "This is a robbery." So for $30 and a carton of cigarettes, he's now facing three years in prison.

He's in jail. We weren't going to bail him out. Then the lawyer told us maybe we should, and get him immediately into rehab. Sometimes the judge is more likely to keep them in rehab, as opposed to putting them in jail. I talked to others who agreed, so that's what we did.

But when he went to his hearing, he pled guilty and then they revoked bail, so then we couldn't get him back into treatment.

Epilogue

I have a hard time talking to him now. I don't know what to say to him. He does talk about program sometimes, but I'm not convinced he's not trying to snow me. He says things, but is he just saying what we want to hear? He says he's sorry and that he's bummed that he can't go to AA meetings. He's in with the hard core inmates because it was a violent felony. He called me and asked me for the recovery house manager's number, which shocked me because he's so stubborn.

I talked to the house manager after he talked to my son, and he said he's never heard him like that – so emotional. He felt like it was sincere.

I don't trust that he's strong. He has a girl friend and that's putting a glitch in our plans. The only way I'll know is when he gets out of jail and starts his life again.

TM – Daughter

My daughter was always a great kid. Always a do-gooder. But between 8th grade and her freshman year of high school it started. She was going through an awkward age where she gained a little weight and I think she had self-esteem issues. Then older guys started paying attention to her.

Being the parent, I was just stupid. I saw her going from being unhappy in 8th grade, to all of a sudden having friends. They were the wrong friends of course, but she was happier and more popular. From freshman, sophomore, junior, and senior year, it was just one bad friend after another. As soon as I would get her away from one, she would go to the next one. They were bad guys – sexually active. From 14 on, it was just downhill from there. Sex, drugs, alcohol…everything.

My daughter was not always getting high or getting drunk. It was just moments: every once in a while. Seriously, about twice a year she would have this explosion of binging. She would try someone's Adderall, come home drunk...it was just a few really bad times.

You turn a blind eye. You think, "Oh she's just doing what we did." It was just an occasional thing.

Then high school freshman year, she started staying away from our house more and more. First it was a sleep over. Then it was Friday and Saturday nights. Then it was the whole weekend and I didn't know where she was.

Then sophomore year we realized something was wrong.

I remember one time in particular. She was going to a beach party and my last words to her were, "Is there going to be any alcohol there?" And she said, "Oh no mom. These are good kids." That night she got arrested for possession.

That was the start of us getting help for her. She got put in a program called "diversion" by the police. It's for kids under 18 who have no prior record. She was assigned a probation officer who interviewed her and me, then set up regular meetings. They provide education on alcohol abuse and had her write a paper about it. She was also required to do a

149

number of hours of community service. If there are no more offenses, then the child's record is cleared.

Of course, what did I do? I helped her all through the program. She did the hours, but I kept pushing her the whole way. I called the places she was doing service. I bugged her all the time about writing the paper. But we don't want to have our kids in trouble right, with a permanent record? I should have just let her fall on her butt. I know now, I should have let her just fail. I was just enabling her to keep on doing what she was doing.

The school also kept calling us and telling us something was up with her. They pulled me in to talk about it. She never cut classes. She was always at school and her grades were decent. She never showed the signs of complete belligerence that many kids do.

She could keep things together for a while, but she was a binger. It was hard to catch her.

Oh yes, my daughter

I want to say, though, that I was never the parent who said, "Not my daughter." I was the one who warned other parents to keep their kids away from her. She would turn the nicest people into kids in trouble.

I was calling up all the parents of her friends and these parents were looking at me like I was completely insane. She would charm them. She could be so sweet. None of those parents were being accountable. It would just fall on deaf ears.

That's when I learned about weekly meetings for families dealing with this from student services at the high school. We were lucky our school had people aware and dealing with teen drug and alcohol problems, instead of in denial. We started with an out-patient group session once a week.

Thank God those meetings were there. My husband (her step dad) and I are a great couple, but those meetings saved us and our sanity. We knew we weren't alone.

Some of the stories you hear in meetings like this may seem over the top, compared to your situation. But you need to listen and then find the ones that you can relate to; look for the similarities and not the differences.

That was sophomore year.

On to IOP

Then in junior year, she didn't come home one night. She got completely wasted and crashed her car. I'd had it by that point and it was time to move to the next step. Through the meetings we'd learned about IOP. We went in for an assessment of her, and she started the program.

She went in kicking and screaming. How does any kid react when they don't think they have a problem? They think that they don't belong there. To her, all the other kids had much worse problems.

You have to be careful not to be drawn into that way of thinking by your kid. We had to get healthy and strong so we didn't believe any of her BS anymore.

She had been admitted a few times to psych hospitals because she was so out of it, but she still couldn't see it. Unfortunately those facilities are insurance driven: they just want to get people in and out of there.

We also put her in psychological counseling, but the counselor was completely on her side. They tell you your child has "feelings", and that they have emotional problems. She didn't even look at the real problem of drug or alcohol abuse.

A professional drug counselor begins to make progress

When we went to IOP, the counselor looked at her as an individual, not with a cookie cutter approach. He can tell after being with them for a while what's happening. He could tell us exactly what's coming and what they're going to do next. A program like that helps you make decisions. You can turn over the reins to someone like that. I was ready to send her away to a residential program, but he said she wasn't ready yet.

Everyone should have a professional counselor to work with. The communication channel is always open between your child and the counselor, even when you don't want to talk to her anymore. She knows she can talk to him. It keeps you sane.

But she also just kept at it. She was dating a drug dealer and that was fine with her. She looked right past his behavior and thought he was a great guy. She had such low self-esteem that she had to go down the totem pole to find guys that were lower than her own self-image. Her rationale was that she knew he was a dealer, but he never did it around her.

We knew that she had to stop seeing him. So my husband told her that. She went ballistic.

From that point on, at 17 years old, she was always staying at friends' houses. Then she went to live with her dad [biological father whom TM divorced].

That's when she crashed her car the second time. She was on her last day of her second go 'round at IOP. She got wasted and took some morphine. She came home just trashed. We had a whole scene in the neighborhood where she kept running out of the house. We had to get in my husband's truck and go track her down. She was walking in the middle of the street in the middle of the night. She was physically fighting us: kicking and biting.

We finally got her in the car and called 911, then took her to a treatment hospital. She was just out of control there too and fighting literally every inch of the way. I didn't recognize her. She was finally transferred from there to a psychiatric hospital in a straight jacket. But they released her within two days. There was never any psychiatric diagnosis.

She was tested for all that when she was younger. In sixth grade she wasn't doing well in school, so the school did a two-week series of tests: psychologists, everything. She was just middle of the road, but there was nothing specific. No ADD, nothing.

She finished high school and actually did OK on her grades. She probably had a 2.7 GPA through it all. She was totally under the radar. She had all the teachers snowed. One even told me, "This girl is so sweet. You must be crazy." They just loved her.

The next year she went away to junior college. But she just was unable to take care of herself. The only way she could exist was if someone else was helping her. She ended up living with someone who did have a diagnosis of bi-polar, but who didn't take her medication. They both started using cocaine heavily.

The problem with girls is that you can't trace it financially. They don't have to pay for their drugs. God only knows how she was getting them. So that was a problem.

Escalating use until she hits bottom for the first time

Then we put software on her computer that tracked everything she was doing. You put it on their computer and your computer, and it lets you use a web browser to track their activity and communications. That's how we found out she was using cocaine.

She made it through just one semester and realized she was in trouble. She wanted to move home, but she wasn't welcome in my house. She moved in with her father. Talk about raising your bottom quickly. Having her move in with your alcoholic ex-husband will do that.

She started dating someone even worse. She was physically abused this time. Beatings, burning her with cigarettes, mental and verbal abuse. The two of them soon started stealing from her father. He had given her the pin numbers for his bank accounts. (Laughs.) They went right to the banks and started taking thousands of dollars. He's financially well off and had no idea for a long time.

At 18, she started dating one of her loser ex-boyfriends and even her father wouldn't put up with that again. He kicked her out.

Within about eight weeks we finally put her in rehab. The only way we got her to go was to take everything from her and give her no other option.

The program was supposed to be 14 months, then within five months she "graduated." That wasn't enough. She was sober for another five months, then started drinking again.

It just wasn't long enough. She bought into the program. She got that she was an addict. It was a 12-step program and she got a sponsor and

153

was working her steps. She went into a sober living environment afterwards. But her sponsor wasn't strong enough. Her sponsor redefined the AA rules for her own purposes: the sponsor's own gambling problems were "under control." So the sponsor thought if my daughter wasn't drinking or using, other bad or irresponsible behaviors were OK.

As a result, my daughter knows she should stay off drugs, but she doesn't believe she's an alcoholic. She's existing and living her life right now, but I think she's still binge drinking.

In her mind, that's not someone who's an alcoholic. She believes she can be a social drinker.

Epilogue

TM's daughter is now a cocktail waitress living in a different city from where she grew up. At the time of this interview, she was about to turn 21 and was planning to go back to school.

TM continues to support her and help her with school because she doesn't want her to come home. Unfortunately, her hope is fading as she sees the same cycle repeating.

Her mother thinks 21 will be a turning point for her, and not in a good way. "I think she's just going to crash hard."

TM's ex-husband is a complicating factor, but generally doesn't fight her plans. He's more than happy to have TM take care of everything, but every once in awhile he'll think he needs to step in. At that point he thinks his words will make everything better, says TM. He tells her, "I've had a talk with her and everything is okay." Unfortunately, he presents the daughter with an option where TM would prefer she had none, because he wants her to come home despite all that she did to him.

TM's advice to others in the same position?

All I can do is verbalize displeasure to my daughter. I tell her all the time that you must realize that if you move back in with dad, it will be the beginning of your next downfall. And that, if you do, I won't have a relationship with you anymore.

What should you do in this situation? The professional line of advice never changes. She must be reminded that her life is not progressing as it should. And not just in terms of her alcoholism. She's still not living a life of integrity in so many ways.

It's strange, but through all this mess they've created, and all the abuse they'll heap on you, they still are seeking your approval. They'll usually listen, even if they don't act on it. Someday the message may sink in.

Continue to provide positive reinforcement, but plan for the worst. You need to constantly plan for whatever your child's next move is, so you know what your corresponding response will be.

Chapter 10 - Stories From Those in Recovery

To preserve the anonymity of those involved, the initials you see here are not the actual initials of these individuals and were chosen at random based on an aspect of their story.

GF – Female

GF certainly had special circumstances that led to her addiction. From a broken home, summer visits to see her alcoholic father led her to begin drinking at age nine. But she also had a relentless mother, who couldn't control her daughter, but did everything she could to keep the pressure on and disrupt GF's alcohol and substance abuse. With limited means and the odds against her, this mother prevailed. GF came to realize that her dad's way – no rules, partying with friends, and doing whatever you want – is not a sustainable lifestyle. Her story offers hope that even very young alcoholics can get clean, change their thinking, and maintain a sober life.

I grew up in Mar Vista, near Los Angeles. I was adopted. My mom would read me these adoption books when I was younger and there would be this baby bird with a family of cows. I knew. I was brown and everyone else was white.

My parents got divorced when I was really young, like six months old. My Dad lived in Texas. And then when I was around nine, my mom and I would go on the bus to his house and she would let me stay there with my dad for the summers.

My dad is a drug addict and alcoholic. I was always interested in what my dad was drinking and it was always Natural Lite beer. And I loved slushies when I was young, so I decided I would make a beer slushy. I thought it was the greatest thing ever. I wanted to be like my dad.

He didn't know at first because he was always drunk. Then as I started getting a little older, that's when we would start drinking together. So in the summer I would drink with my dad and my mom wouldn't know.

I just wanted to be like my dad. With my mom I had to follow rules, but with my dad I could stay up as long as I wanted, stay out late, watch scary movies…anything I wanted. He was always happy and it didn't seem like he had any type of lifestyle he had to live by.

I went to a private school from kindergarten to sixth grade. But in junior high, seventh grade, my mom had to send me to a public school. She was just a single parent and my dad didn't help her with money at all. So she couldn't afford to send me to this really expensive school that all my friends went to. I went to a public school in a very affluent area and that's when it got worse for me.

From the outside view there was really nothing wrong. It was a really nice area. All the homes were really big. It was a great school. But it was a charter school, so we had kids coming from every area of the city. Just a bunch of people from all different cultures and homes put together. Everything from inner-city gangs to rich kids.

I was smoking weed and doing cocaine. When I would go see my dad I would bring cocaine and me and my dad would do it together. It was really bad. My mom had an idea, but she really never knew for sure what I was doing.

Finally I came out and told my mom, "Dad's better. I have much more fun when I'm with him." She told me I couldn't go see him anymore. I said alright, that's fine, I'm just going to drink and use here. So I did, with my friends.

In eighth grade it just got worse. I started doing meth and heroin, and I got kicked out of school. None of the other high schools around there would accept me. At that point I began to go in and out of mental hospitals. I wasn't eating and was really underweight and unhealthy.

I've been in counseling since I was about eight. I had bad nightmares so I've been in therapy since I was little. It never really helped because I never opened up to anyone. The very first therapist I had, I wasn't willing to open up. Throughout my life I've probably had 25 therapists; every year it changed.

I developed this huge fear of getting close to anyone because I'd have to start over. I'd tell them things, then I'd have to start over with a new one. I created friendships at school, then I'd have to go to a new school and start all over. It was like starting over, over and over again.

So in ninth grade the school didn't want me anymore. I was fighting other kids and just barely attending classes.

With wrong choices, life is a mess

I didn't really think about what I was doing. I knew I wanted to be like my dad. At the time my dad got to work when he wanted. He got to party all the time with friends. He had just one TV, one table and a couch. To me that was the greatest thing ever.

I could get any movie I wanted. I could stay up all night. I could eat all the candy I wanted. My dad seemed happy and free spirited.

My dad had a business where he didn't go to work regular hours. He could make his own schedule. I don't know how he did it, but I'd go to work with him sometimes. People would call and he would go do what he did. I don't know how much he got paid, but it was enough to make a living and have his apartment.

His whole family drank, so my aunts and uncles, my grandparents were all big drinkers. Drinking was just something that was a part of life.

But my mom was like, okay you spilled something, you have to clean it up right now, right away. Everything has to be tidy and neat. It was from one extreme to the other.

With my mom's family, they don't drink. They were really loud, like a New York Italian family. They would argue over little things. Yelling was a part of conversation.

My life became a mess. Putting that all together was just a mess for me. I had a lot of friends, you know, I knew a lot of people. But as far as the real meaning of a friend, I had maybe one or two. Then I ruined those friendships because of my drinking and using.

A persistent mom gets GF's recovery started

So I was just in and out of mental hospitals and then, when I got expelled again and no school would take me, my mom sent me to a recovery facility in Utah.

My mom got the state to pay. My mom was a trooper. She definitely did a lot of things for me. There's a point where parents just give up. My mom was denied on a lot of things she tried to do. She just kept asking people, "What do I do? My daughter is out of control."

My mom was a great parent. She taught me right from wrong and she worked hard. She raised me in a good home. She would sleep in front of the door so I wouldn't get out. But ultimately, what was she going to do? She couldn't hit me. She never did hit me or anything. She was just at a point where she didn't know what to do anymore. She was so afraid I was going to end up dead and of getting that phone call from the police or something.

A lot of people told her there's nothing you can do. You're going to have to send her to a continuation high school. My mom did the research on continuation schools and that is just a bunch of bad kids collected from one area.

So she applied for a state grant program called AB3632 [mental health services for students with disabilities]. The rehab that I went to was like $450 a day. My mom didn't have the money and I went there twice. But the state said they would pay for me. They transferred me from a mental hospital to the program in Utah.

Break them down to build them up

Utah was like a jail/rehab. It was a lockdown facility. I was 14 when I got there. You had to earn everything. You had earn the right to go to the bathroom by yourself. You had to check in all the time with someone who had been there for a longer time. There are different levels of facilities and this was a Level 14 lockdown. [Residential Treatment Facilities are given a rating for the level of care they provide. Level 14 is the highest level on the scale.] It was just a step down from juvenile hall.

160

You couldn't wear the clothes you wanted. At first you had to wear sweats. They pretty much broke me down. I really had to humble myself and they taught me everything all over again. Self-respect, respect for property, being grateful for what you have. There was no cussing. I would complain about everything. I had to earn the right to have a phone call with my mom and to go outside in a little caged-in area.

It was an all-girl school. Once you raised your status level, you would earn some trust. You would get to go out with other girls. If you did something you would have to wear a sign around your neck like, "My name is [GF] and I have an attitude problem. How can I tell you what your problem is when I can't focus on myself?"

They would give short term detention. If you cussed or did something wrong you would get points assigned to you. To work off your points, you had to sit in a chair with your feet on the ground and your hands folded, and for every half an hour it would take two points off your total.

Every hour you got a five minute break to go to the bathroom or get a drink. If you leaned back or didn't keep your hands folded, you wouldn't get your points for that half hour. So it was all up to you and when you were willing to serve your time as a consequence of what you did. It was really intense.

I was there for about a year. For the first four months I faked it and said I want to be there and do everything right. But I was trying to write my old friends. My counselor found out and that cost me all my status.

They had meetings there and they would take you out to [AA] meetings too. They had different counseling groups for drugs, alcohol, eating disorders, body image stuff, how to take care of yourself and defend yourself from rape. All kinds of groups for everything you can imagine.

Eventually I stayed and graduated the program. It was a great school. I thought I was ready to be done drinking and using. Me and my mom had built a great relationship. She had come and visited me many times. I had home visits where I flew home too.

Letting her program slip   **restarts trouble back home**

161

When I got home my mom wrote a contract that we agreed to. I had to keep my bed made and do chores. I only did it for a few weeks.

The only school I could go to was a continuation school. I was sober, but I knew it was going to be really hard. My mom knew this was a fork in the road. She wanted what was best for me, so she had them set up a special program for me. I could leave class whenever I wanted. I could have my cell phone on campus so I could call my mom or someone sober if I got in a bad situation.

This was in a deep ghetto area of Los Angeles. I was around a bunch of gang bangers. I was probably back for only about two weeks and I just started drinking and using again.

They had taxis pick us up to take us to school. Everyone in my taxi was using. We went through at least eight taxi drivers. People would burn the seats or tag their seats. I was in the car with people doing lines of drugs on the back of their school books and bringing rum in a juice box. I could only be around it so long before I caved in.

I wasn't working a program. I wasn't doing the steps. I didn't have a sponsor. So I was completely on my own trying to stay sober. That doesn't work.

My mom was trying to control everything. I would tell her I felt like drinking and using. I wasn't going to, but she didn't know how to handle that. I felt like I couldn't go to her and talk about how I was struggling. She would freak out. It was understandable. But being as young as I was, I needed someone to talk to.

I was going to meetings and I had a sponsor. But I was lying and was getting loaded with people in the program and I wasn't talking to my sponsor. My mom would drop me off at my sponsor's house. I would pretend I was going to go in, but then tell my sponsor a lie, like "I can't be here. I just stopped by to say hello." Then I'd get picked up by someone else.

I was out for six months and I was down to 85 pounds: I'm normally about 120. My drugs of choice were meth and heroin. I combined the two. I was awake for so long. I had meth blackouts and I was seeing things like they were real. I could see myself killing people I knew.

The final steps to recovery

I came out of this meth blackout one time and I was standing over my mom's body with a knife in my hands. My mom woke up and freaked out. She called 911 and they took me to the mental hospital. I was crying and told them just to do whatever they had to do to help me. I knew I really needed help and I didn't want to use.

They transferred me to a regular hospital because I was coming down [from the drugs] and had to be watched. After I was there a few days I went back to the psych hospital. That was my fourth or fifth time being there, so they knew me. But I told them I was there because I needed to be and I wanted help.

My mom was able to get me back to Utah and the state was willing to pay for me again.

After that, I was really honest with my mom about everything that was going on. I was more honest than I've ever been. So I went back when I was 16 and stayed there about eight months. It was really embarrassing. All the girls that had been there the last time that I was there, that had looked up to me when I left, were still there.

My mom was by my side the whole time. She asked if I needed anything. On visits she would pick me up and take me places and sit in parking lots while I went to meetings. She even said if I have to smoke cigarettes, she didn't like it, but if that was going to stop me from doing anything else, then do whatever you need to do.

She was there as much as she could be. My dad only talked to me once or twice while I was in rehab. He would always bail out when I would call because he was still drinking and doing heroin. It was off and on when he would show up and when he wouldn't be there.

I got honest about a lot of things. I had the same counselor and he told me that we would pick up where we left off. We just needed to do more work and touch on a lot more fears and a lot more defects, and a lot more of what was the root of what was going on with me.

I graduated high school at 16. I had a choice to stay a few more months in Utah and graduate in rehab or leave after five or six months and graduate back at home. I thought maybe I could go back and do all of the things I was supposed to do. Or I could graduate in rehab and then just go on to college.

My old high school was old people and old places and that takes you back to the old you. The only part of me that wanted to go back there was the part of me that wanted to use. So I decided it wasn't a good idea for me.

But Utah was a great place. I was doing things I used to do. We had a soccer team and I had grown up playing club soccer. I was taking voice lessons and I sang at my graduation. I started to become myself again. I was healthy and was on the right path.

I graduated and was out about two weeks. Again, I thought I was done. It was August of 2007.

One Last Slip

So I hung out with one of my friends and went into the situation saying to myself, "I'm not going to drink. I'm not going to use." This guy said, no it's cool we don't have to drink or use. Then he was like, "there's nothing to do. Want to go get some Vodka?" And I said sure. We went to the liquor store and bought it. Then I said, okay, I'll only have one sip. Just one.

The next thing I know, I woke up in the hospital with GHB ["date rape" drug] in my system and alcohol poisoning.

My mom was crying. Again, she was wondering what she was doing wrong.

That's the last time that I drank or used. My sobriety date is August 29, 2007. It definitely was something that was really hard. I decided that I wasn't going to NA (narcotics anonymous) because that's where I got into trouble before. I went to AA.

I wasn't really an alcoholic. My deal was drugs. My mom said, just replace alcohol in my mind with drugs. So I tried it and went to my first young people's AA meeting with my mom. I was scared and didn't like it at first, but I saw all these young people that I could relate too. They shared their stories.

The next night I went to a women-only meeting. I ended up getting a sponsor. My mom and I also began to create a better relationship. I was like the boy who cried wolf. I was like, "I'm done, no I'm not. I'm done, I'm going to drink. No wait, I'm done. I swear."

Finally looking ahead

Now I'm 20 years old and just took a three year chip. My mom is my best friend. I can talk to her about absolutely anything. My friends come over and they love her and she loves my friends.

Every now and then she struggles with still trying to control some things in my life. There were a few months where I didn't have a job and I wasn't willing to get off my butt and do anything about it. My mom was asking me what I was doing with my life. And we didn't get along for awhile. But she was right and we've gotten along for most of my sobriety.

When I had a little over a year sober, I went to make amends to all my friends and family in Texas. My dad was good then and was trying to be sober. His parents had died from alcohol, of liver disease. I made amends to my dad and some of my cousins.

I also met my dad's fiancé. Then my dad told me that was the last time he could talk to me because the fiancé made him choose her or me. I don't know what her problem is. My dad and I haven't talked in a couple of years.

My mom has been like my mom and dad. Through all this, my mom has stood by my side. My mom never kicked me out. It was me running away because I didn't want to listen to the rules.

I'm working and I'm going to go back to school soon. I went to junior college for a year and a half, but I stopped to go see my cousin in Utah. She's struggling with addiction right now. I was there for a couple of months. I felt like it was something I needed to do.

I still live with my mom. I just need a few more credits and then I'll be done with community college. I either want to go to a university or go and get my CAADAC (California Association of Alcoholism and Drug Abuse Counselors). It's a nine-month program.

I still go to meetings and I still have a sponsor. My mom and I go to Al-Anon meetings every once in a while. She's not an Al-Anon regular but she'll come with me sometimes. We're pretty good about separating our programs.

Our big thing now is listening and trying to understand the other person; placing ourselves in the other person's shoes and trying to hear what they are really saying.

RH – Male

I always had problems with authority. I hated rules and I hated having to listen to and mind adults, especially ones who I thought weren't very smart. And of course I thought I was smarter than just about everyone. Basically I was a d**k to any authority figure in my life.

So I was in trouble at school from a very young age. I would speak out in class and did not respect my teachers, or again, just about any adult in charge. I challenged them on everything. My parents told me over and over again that sometimes you just have to be quiet and be one of the crowd, whether you agree with it or not, but I just couldn't do that.

My teachers knew I was pretty smart. I was always in the gifted and AP programs. They would always say something like, "You know your son is a very bright boy, but…" Then they would get into all my behavioral problems.

But I didn't want to be one of the smart kids. Ever since I can remember, I always wanted to hang out with the "bad boys." It was way more fun. My mom will tell you that from a very young age, I was difficult. Not warm and cuddly.

With that attitude I was in trouble a lot, but it really started getting more crazy in middle school. My friends and I started this gang, or club, or whatever you want to call it. You had to be kind of a troublemaker to be in it. I don't even want to get into the details. But one key thing was, you could never rat any of the other guys out. We had this strict rule that if you got in trouble and got called to the office or had to talk to your parents about anything that happened, you could never tell on any other kid. You just took your punishment or whatever they decided to do. So the secrecy and lying started then.

And honestly, I didn't care about consequences, punishment or restriction at all. I would either just "serve my time," or just say screw it, and find a way to get around it.

Behavior escalates in middle school

So in middle school we started doing stupid stuff just to have fun. We started sneaking out at night. Our house was a two-story and my bedroom was at the front of our house. All I had to do was take the screen off the window, climb onto the roof and climb down a wall at the corner of the garage. Then I was gone.

One night a friend and I "camped out" in a tent in our back yard, but of course we didn't sleep. We got up and hopped the fence. We used to do crazy stuff at night. One of my friends was pretty well off and they had a top-of-the-line BMW. We used to sneak it out of his garage and drive it all over the place in the middle of the night. We got that thing up to 100 mph on the freeway. No license. And we were high or drunk most of the time. I did it one time with my brother's car too. It's amazing we never got caught or killed ourselves.

Getting into the schools was another thing we did. We'd go swimming in the high school pool. We drove an electric cart around the high school. Or climb onto the roofs and screw around or vandalize stuff. Several of my friends got caught for stuff, but I usually didn't. Lots of fun back then. That's what your kids are probably doing.

It was around then, at 14 years old, that I first started drinking and smoking weed.

The first time my parents started to do something about it was when one of my friends - one who didn't use - told his parents that he knew I was smoking. His dad called my dad and told him what he had heard about me. That's really when my parents started paying attention.

I was in trouble so much that it was probably harder for them than some other kid who was good all the time, then starts using and gets an attitude. At first, they couldn't tell what were the effects of the drugs and what was just my sucky attitude in general.

Eventually more stuff started happening. I was supposed to be doing homework, but I was spending time on the computer hooking up with friends to go get high. And that was even though I never had a TV or computer in my room.

My parents would check my grades online and there would be tons of zeros because I wasn't turning in my homework. At first, I would still pull my grades out at the end because school was pretty easy for me.

My brother went off to college when I started high school. I went to visit him and we got high and drank beer there. My parents had talked to him, but he didn't get that I wasn't like him. I didn't really get it then either, that I was an addict. I wasn't just messing around with it like he was.

My high school was watching me too. I was on the freshman baseball team and one coach in particular could see who I was hanging out with. He thought I was wasting my talent, which I was. He would confront me about it, but I would blow him off. We also had a woman who was in student services who was dedicated to finding out who was screwing around and trying to get them into programs to stop.

She could see what was going on with me and called my parents in for a conference. She sat there and told them I was a pot head, that it was well known at school and my parents needed to do something about it. I remember just sitting there. I didn't talk. I thought she was a total b**ch. But that's when my parents got me into a program for the first time. They started drug testing me too.

First we went to a meeting once a week at a drug treatment facility. A bunch of the people I hung out with were there too. We would all sit in a circle and the counselor would call people out and have them tell why they were there. I had to go there for eight weeks or something like that. They would yell at us and try to get us to think about what we were doing. But we didn't get it at all. I didn't care what they said. Just get me through the meetings and let me do what I want.

We didn't stop. I found ways to get around the drug tests. Or I would swear that the test must be wrong. They used home tests at first, where you had to send the specimen off to this lab to be verified if it showed positive. That just bought me time to go hang out with my friends and get high more.

Playing the game against the parents

My whole thing was to play my mom and dad against each other. My mom was hard core, but my dad always wanted to believe me. I would make it a point to ask my dad first if I could. If he said I could go somewhere, then I would take off or have him take me there before my mom found out.

They tried to do the right thing, like meeting my friends' parents. There were a couple of those parents who would put up a good front, but they were using too! Or the parents wouldn't pay attention enough, so we could get out and smoke or whatever, even if they didn't approve.

There were certain friends who my parents trusted. A lot of those friends, I got high with too. Or I would have my mom or dad take me to the "good friend's" house, hang out there for a little bit, then move on to my using buddies. And if they put me on restriction, I would sneak out. Until my dad figured out what I was doing and screwed the screens into the window frames.

I came home one time and was trying to get in and my dad caught me. He knew by then. When I climbed down he said, "You've been up there before, huh?" I knew that was over. He found smudges from my shoes where I was climbing from our front porch up to the roof. Later they moved me to another bedroom in the house and it was like a two story drop from my window then. We had one of those folding fire escape ladders and I thought more than once about using that thing to get out at night. That's how crazy I was to go get high.

Once I could get a little of their trust back, I would just take advantage of that. One thing I did when I still had my cell phone was, at night, just before they would go to bed, I would say that I was going to the garage to talk to my girlfriend on the phone. I told them I wanted to go in there so it would be private and so I wouldn't disturb them. So they wouldn't lock the door or turn on the alarm. Of course I was totally lying to them. That gave me a clean way to go smoke or go out and be with my friends.

Looking back, it's hard to believe they went for that. But parents want to believe you, so naturally kids are going to exploit that any way they can.

They tried to limit my TV and computer time, but I would find ways to chisel away at the new rules and eventually get to do most of what I wanted. Of course I would never follow any of the rules if they weren't around to enforce them, and I would always try to get around them for some stupid reason.

It didn't matter what my parents did. I told all kinds of stories. I lied right to their faces. I was really good at it. I covered up the smell of pot or alcohol with Axe spray(cologne) or women's perfume. Girls would give it to me. I chewed lots of spearmint gum.

We would hide our drugs in a canyon near my house.

With more frequency, it starts catching up to RP

Eventually I was caught one too many times. Mainly because I was doing it more and more. It was bound to happen. One time my dad came to get me at 10 or 11 and took me home. We had an alarm on the house, but there was a skinny window in a downstairs bathroom with no alarm on it. I squeezed my way through it, but fell and made a bunch of noise knocking over some trash cans. I was already drunk. He chased me in the car and I tried to hide, but he made me get in the car and come home. I told him there were girls at the party and that's why I was going back. Somehow that made him feel better so I didn't get in as much trouble as I might have.

We also went on this snowboard trip. It was promoted at the school, but wasn't connected with it. It was basically some college guys who set up tours to snow resorts in the winter and places like Cancun in the spring. They would give a high school kid a free tour to promote it within the schools. Of course they said it would be supervised and drug free. What a joke. The whole thing was designed so a bunch of kids could go away for the week, get high, get drunk, and hook up with each other. And that's what we did.

Before we left to come home from the trip I was able to buy a case of beer and I drank them all, one-by-one on the 10-hour bus ride home. I had the perfect excuse when I got home. I was totally drunk, but I told my parents I was just really, really tired from the trip so I could sleep it off.

For parents, if you want to protect your kids, don't ever let them go on one of those tours. Especially for girls. I guarantee you those college guys running the whole thing were using it as a way to hook up with high school girls.

Another time I was out in a car with a bunch of friends and the cops stopped us. We had pot in the car and could have been arrested. But the police didn't want to do the paperwork or go through the hassle of taking us to juvenile hall, so they just called my parents to come get me. I could have been arrested a bunch of times, but I always just got away with things, so that made me even more bold.

An attempt to quit

I actually did stop for a while and was clean for about six months when I was in the 10th grade. One of my best friends got sent away to a wilderness residential drug program in Montana. That shook me up for the first time. I was in the once-a-week group meeting and was getting drug tested. I wanted to play baseball, so I tried to stay clean. I started working out for baseball and acting better at home.

But I kept hanging out with my old friends and so of course I got back into it. You don't just hang out and watch other guys smoke or get high. This time it was worse and I started smoking every day. I didn't want to do anything but hang out with friends and get wasted. This time around, I didn't do the off-season baseball conditioning program and got cut from the team in the spring of my junior year. By the end of my junior year my grades started to tank. I made it to summer and it was on.

It was mainly pot, but we were trying other things too, like ecstasy and prescription drugs. Some cocaine too. We took weed smoking to an art form. I made my own pipe from stuff in my dad's garage. One of my friends even made a bong from a WWII gas mask. We shot videos of us using that one.

My parents eventually found the video on my cell phone. They started checking my phone for the call history and who I was texting. Also for any pictures or videos. Of course I was all pissed off, saying they were violating my privacy. But they did pay for the phone and I was still a minor, so why wouldn't they do that?

So in October of my senior year in high school, I went back into the IOP program. I still wasn't down to get sober. I couldn't imagine not getting high. What else would you do? I hated the counselor, but I just tried to get through it so I could get back to baseball and get my parents to back off a little.

I had to find ways to get around the drug tests too. In the program, they use the heavy duty tests through a hospital. It registers your levels, not just positive or negative. My levels weren't going down.

There are also lots of ways to mess with drug tests so you don't have a positive. We used niacin, which flushes out your system. You can drink lots of water before a test to dilute it or put stuff into the cup like salt, vinegar, detergent…anything that will screw with the test. Kids also sell each other clean pee. I didn't do much of that. I just BS'd my way through and tried to convince them that the stuff in my system was from the times before I quit.

So that worked for a while but then in December of my senior year, I didn't do one of the assignments for my program. As a consequence of that, my counselor assigned me a two-page essay and I just decided that I was not going to do it.

I remember my dad was driving me home from the meeting that day and I was just telling him that it was BS and wasn't fair and that I was not going to do it. He knew that meant I would be kicked out of the program and then he and my mom would have to follow through with their threats. He was upset and tried to plead with me to really think about what I was doing.

I wasn't going to change my mind. I even told him if they wanted to take me out of baseball, then have at it, because I was going to do things my own way. I remember going to a meeting later that week too and just sitting there telling everyone that I was not going to do it and they could take whatever steps they thought they needed to after that. This one woman was yelling at me about how stupid it was. Of course they could see what was going to happen and cared about me, but I just thought they were hassling me. I was way too smart for them, right?

"I'm 18 and can do what I want"

173

I really thought I was going to be fine. My 18th birthday was coming in a few months and I thought that was going to be my "emancipation." I'd get away from my parents and live my own life. I'd explain to anyone who would listen that I wasn't like other kids who would keep going into more heavy drugs. I'd done my research online. Marijuana was a natural plant and was not addictive or a gateway to other drugs. I was thinking, I like it, tons of people do it, there's nothing wrong with it, and I could manage my life just fine.

So my parents at this point were finally done with me. They told me to stay in the program or I was moving to the garage. They took all my stuff away and moved it into their bedroom where they could lock it up. Video games, clothes, cell phone – everything – and put me in the garage with a couple of blankets. I got to go into the house to go to the bathroom and get ready for school. They would even bring my meals out to me.

I was pissed. We had big fights. I said they were treating me worse than the dog, since he got to sleep in the house – trying to make them feel guilty. I got mad and punched out one of the garage door windows one time. I had already put holes in a couple of walls in the house just to show them they couldn't control me. I even broke the door to their bedroom to try and get in to get my stuff. Me and my parents fought all the time and I would cuss them out for not letting me make my "lifestyle choices."

I wasn't changing, so my parents said I had to leave the house when I turned 18. I thought that was cool. I had a place I knew I could go stay. The day before my birthday my parents let me pack up some clothes in a suitcase. The next day my mom drove me to school and left me across the street with my stuff.

Reaching the bottom

I had a friend who lived near the school and his family was going to let me stay in their garage. His parents were Christians – one was ordained as a minister – and they didn't believe in trying to control their kids' behavior. They thought the stuff that went on in the meetings I went to was humiliating and wrong. They preached unconditional love. I thought that was great; just what I was looking for. They thought their kids were just experimenting, and would be fine if they just supported them, loved them, and prayed about it.

What they didn't know was that both their sons were drug dealers to the community, and way deeper into drugs than they thought.

From that day, everything got worse. What I thought would be the best thing, turned out to not be anything like I imagined. Since I was 18 and an adult now, I figured I could go play baseball and my parents couldn't do anything about it. I would be able to call myself out of school when I wanted. I could go get a job and start to pay rent. Because of my SAT scores, I was already accepted to three universities. Maybe I could even go to college. I'd show everyone.

Instead my drug and alcohol use got worse and really started to ruin my life. My baseball coach would not let me back on the team because he promised my parents that if I wasn't in a program, I couldn't play. Of course now that I had the choice, I wasn't going to go to school, so my grades went to s***. I didn't really even try to get a job.

Instead I got my dad to give me my Xbox back and went and sold it to buy drugs and pay rent. Part of the money was supposed to be my "seed money" so I could start selling with my friends. Then I could pay rent. Instead I used all the drugs I bought. I started using new stuff like mushrooms. It got so bad I would drink and use until I passed out every night and wake up the next morning with my pants soaked in my own urine.

I started to see that this was not going the way I had hoped, so I tried to bargain with my parents. I still didn't get how serious they were.

I went to the same lady in student services at the high school that had got me started in the program and asked her to get my parents to come to the school for a meeting. They came, but they had a contract with them that outlined everything they wanted me to do if I came home. Of course that included getting clean. I tried to bargain with them, but by this time they were a unified front, so they would not back down at all. I was crying and really messed up, but I wasn't ready to change then, so I went back to the friend's house again.

At some point just after that, I was walking home from school and my dad was sitting in the car waiting for me. He asked me to talk with him. He told me about a residential drug recovery program that he and my mom had found. They had been up to visit it and thought it was the right place for me. He told me that this would be something I could do on my own, and it would take him and my mom out of the whole equation, so we wouldn't have to worry about going back to the same old family conflicts. He said he would pay for it if I was interested and to please think about it.

From fun to desperation

My using and drinking were really bad now. I was a full blown addict/alcoholic. And something strange was happening. It just wasn't fun anymore. I would find myself hanging out with these loser kids every day. One even stole a bunch of stuff from us – supposedly his friends. And I believe I heard God speaking to me. He was telling me that this was wrong, that I was wasting my life, and that I needed to get help.

I tried one more time to get my parents to let me come home. We went out to the office of this psychologist that is like 20 miles from our house. Again my parents showed up with the behavior contract and said this is what I needed to do. I told them I was willing to negotiate. Wrong move. Meeting over.

They had given me a ride to this place, so I figured I was going to show them they still couldn't control me. I refused to buckle my seat belt in the car. My dad told me either buckle it or get out. I didn't believe they would follow through. They did. I remember chucking a water bottle at the back of the car as they drove away without me.

Finally, late in my senior year, I found out I was going to fail my English class and that I would not be able to graduate. I was in class and I was freaking out. I had always been able to pull my grades out somehow, but not this time. The teacher would not back down, thank God. Even some of the other kids in the class were in my face, telling me how screwed up I was and to do something about it. Everyone could see how I was wasting my life except me and my drug buddies. I think that was my "hitting bottom" that everyone talks about.

That day was a Wednesday and I knew my dad worked at home on Wednesdays. I walked straight from school to my house. When my dad came to the door I said, "Dad, is that offer of help still open, because I think I'm ready."

That night, my dad drove me up to LA near the recovery house and we spent the night in a hotel. My mom was freaked out. She was worried that I was going to steal my dad's wallet and car and take off, but my dad said later that he was cool and never really thought about it. The next morning we went to the recovery house and that was the beginning of the best thing that ever happened to me.

"Brain washed"

I'm going on three years sober now. I always thought that these recovery houses would brain wash you and make you this clone of everyone else. Actually they do some brain washing because your brain needs to be washed after all the drugs and other crap you've put into it. But really, I'm a lot the same as I always was. They get into your character defects like a good program should, but in general I still have a lot of my same personality. But now I'm living without drugs and alcohol.

It takes time and a lot of work, so you really have to be ready to do it. These 30 or 60 day programs; I mean, you can get clean, but it doesn't really change you. It takes months to change your thinking and behavior. I was using for four years so you're not going to change all that in 30 days. Now I'm living with integrity and think about other people, not just myself.

About two months before I graduated my program though, I was messing up again. Not using, but just slipping back into some old habits and getting lazy with my program work. The consequences that the house put on me made me think for a minute that I might just say screw it. But eventually, I just couldn't go back to the way it was before. There just isn't anything good about it.

Now I am supporting myself 100%. I have a good job and live in a cool apartment close to the beach. I've got lots of great friends that will do anything for me. Real friends and real relationships, not ones based on using or what you can do for me.

I have my family back too. We've shared some great times in the past three years. We have really good conversations and can enjoy each other now. Of course it's not perfect. Of course life isn't perfect. But I've been taught through my program that that's OK. I know how to deal with it now.

Lessons for parents

The biggest thing, and the hardest thing, is to try to back off from your emotional reaction. You want to believe your kids. You think you can talk to them and make them better. You think they won't lie. But they do lie and it just doesn't work that way, so dealing with teenagers is different from dealing with a 10 year-old.

Stick to what you believe. Enforce your rules and don't let your kids chip away at them. Because we will, and before you know it, your rules and standards will be so low you won't know what happened. And then we're running the house.

Mainly you need to stick with it. You need to keep after them. Young teenagers usually don't get it. Their brains just don't work in a rational way. They can sit in the meetings, but they can't look ahead and say, "I shouldn't do these drugs because they could hurt me in the long run." But that doesn't mean you should stop trying. The more you stir things up and put the pressure on, the closer you get to getting them to quit screwing themselves up. You may not see it when you're in the middle of it, but it is having an effect.

It took my parents, especially my dad, awhile to see that. But eventually they came together and there was no way for me to keep doing the same stupid stuff. They just got tough and would not back down. They didn't leave me any alternative. It was either get in a program and change, or keep hanging out with losers and watch my life go down the toilet.

I'm lucky they got tough on me. They stuck with me when I didn't deserve it. I thank them for that.

VY – Male

I didn't really have good grades growing up. I was failing out most of my years. It got a little better in middle school, but then fell again in high school. I basically just went to school and went home. I didn't do any extracurricular activities.

My difficulties really started pretty young. In second grade my teacher told my parents I'd have problems if I continued to do my schoolwork the way I was doing. I had bad grades and got in trouble for behavior issues.

In sixth grade my parents sent me to a psychologist. I had been diagnosed with ADHD and they wanted to put me on Adderall. They thought that was the problem with my lack of focus at school. We did that for a while, but the medicine made me sick to my stomach so they took me off it. I went to three other psychologists after that – all for ADHD.

None of it really helped. I'd go and wouldn't really talk that much. I'd go get a burger and go home.

It continued that way until seventh grade, when I started using. Then it just got worse from there.

The first time I used was with one of my friends from school. We were at the skate park and we smoked weed.

I didn't sneak out to do it. It was just go out, do it, and then veg at home. I wouldn't really do anything all day, or I would be out of the house all day, so it really wasn't a problem at home.

My family was definitely an upper middle class family in a nice neighborhood. Both parents in the home. My dad retired when I was about 13 or 14, so he was home a lot with me.

My parents first knew something was going on after my eighth grade year. I was using like once a week to twice a month up until that summer when I started using every day, sometimes twice a day. It stayed that way through freshman year of high school. All weed at that point.

My grades had dropped. It took a while and they didn't really jump on it. It was more hinting at it since my grades were bad and my attitude wasn't as good as it used to be. They checked into who I was hanging out with, but I knew really sneaky kids who could get around that.

My friends changed over the years. Kids would get changed to new districts or new schools. Or we'd just switch to new groups of kids.

We'd make up all kinds of lies. We'd start at the "least bad" kid's house, then go from there to the next person's house, then to the next and so on, collecting more kids as we went.

We wouldn't go home and, even if it meant staying out an extra hour, we'd make up some huge story about how something had happened and that's why we were late. We'd play off that story and make sure we each knew what we were going to say so that we could get away with it to each parent.

I had a cell phone, but I didn't use that too much to contact people because my parents read my text messages. There wasn't any way to track me through the phone except for the numbers I called. But I could always put the phone numbers under someone else's name…that made it look like it was one of my "good" friends to throw them off the track.

Whenever I saw my parents, I'd have conflicts with them. When I was home, I never left my room. I would just go outside and smoke, then watch TV all day in my room. It was to the point that when I would talk to them, it was, "F*** you. You're not my parents." [VY was adopted] I was treating them like trash. I would leave the house and not come home – sleeping at someone else's house.

I would come home during the week and go to school, but I didn't really do anything at school. Yet I'd complain about how hard school was, then leave again.

Parents' action, and professional help, begin the path to recovery

They probably let me out of the house too much and didn't pay attention to what I was doing. Once they really attacked it, it was half way through my sophomore year. They started drug testing me. I failed three tests and they sent me to an IOP.

My parents restricted me when I didn't do my homework or wasn't home on time. I'd lose my TV and Xbox privileges. They were things I could easily live without for a while, then I'd go back to doing the same things. That just repeated itself, but it stopped when I went into the program because it was more concrete then.

Once they started the drug tests I stopped for about two months and then I started again. When they first started testing me, it was because I had tried ecstasy. So I got spooked off that. And they threatened to send me to a rehab, so I just stopped for awhile. Then they said they were going to send me to an in-patient, hospital program anyway, so I started using again. But once I knew I was going into the program [IOP], I stopped again.

My parents called and talked to a counselor, and I talked to him on the phone. He could tell I was resistant to it. They took me to his office and he told us what was going to happen. We started three days a week in the IOP.

At the time I just sort of shut down. I wasn't willing to cooperate with it, but I wasn't going to cause problems.

After about eight weeks in IOP I decided I was going to run away [at 15 years old]. I wasn't really happy with it. I left right after school on a Friday. I took a bus to [a city about 25 miles south of here] and stayed there for the night. Then I went to another city just south of there and stayed there for two nights. Then me and some friends I met there went to a rave.

The rave scene

At raves, about half of the people are there for the music, but about half are there for the drugs and the scene that goes with it. Girls wear tutus...it's mainly dress like a hooker day for them. As skimpy as possible. Guys go in tank tops and shorts. Everyone wears candy bracelets and necklaces. People will use pacifiers and Vick's rub. They inhale the menthol which is supposed to heighten the experience when you're on ecstasy.

The colors of the clothes are really bright, fluorescent. Some people buy glow sticks that they like to flail around. They also enhance the visual effects of the drugs. Kids wear gloves too. Most just buy the sticks to look cool and play with.

The rave we went to was at a family entertainment/miniature golf place so it was really open. The organizer had told the owners that only about 50 people would come, so they said it was fine because they needed the business. Then about 500-600 people showed up and that's when the cops came.

I had been to about three raves at that point. We had taken ecstasy two hours into it. Then the police busted it. I got caught and arrested there.

Arrest is a catalyst for change

Everyone was bailing, but they found me in a parking lot where me and some of my friends were talking. They took me down to the station, but didn't hold me. They gave me a blood test, but let me go because juvy didn't have any room and my parents were there.

My parents took me straight to a hospital and I stayed there four days to detox. I got charged with being under the influence of methamphetamine [a common ingredient in ecstasy]. I got six months informal probation, which means my parents were my probation officer. They made me do three months in a program plus AA meetings each week and 40 hours of community service.

Once I got home I agreed to go back to the IOP.

When I ran away, it was way too hard. I knew I wouldn't have made it if I wasn't found on that fourth day. I had no money; no place to live. I was just going to sleep under a bridge somewhere. I just knew I had to go through the group if I was going to survive on my own someday.

My parents didn't work with me at all then. Whenever I would talk to them, they wouldn't talk back. They would just say, "Talk to your counselor." At one point I had just a blanket on my floor in my room; that was it. No door. No furniture. I had had a computer in my room. I would always be on either MySpace or Facebook talking to people, setting things up like parties and other stuff. That got moved back out to the family room. My parents took my cell phone too.

Working for recovery

I'm 17 and coming up on six months clean now. I have just a few more meetings and a few hours left on my probation. Even when it's done, it won't change that much. My parents will still have me doing pretty much the same stuff.

When I was using, people would tell me things and I wouldn't pay attention, but I talked to them like I knew what they were saying. After getting off it, I had really bad anxiety and paranoia. I thought I could hear people outside my room or the house, coming to get me.

Is weed addictive? Physically no, mentally yes. There's no physical withdrawals, but it's all mental where you need it to function and "be yourself." My brain was pretty messed up and it took a long time for that to go away. Maybe six months.

[We can't help but interject here. Think about that cliché phrase "mentally yes, but physically no" for awhile. Is your brain part of your physical being? Uh, yeah. In fact it is the most complex organ in your body.

Dr. Joe Dispenza, in his book *Evolve The Brain; The Science of Changing Your Mind*, describes how the brain's proper chemical balance and ability to fire impulses across tens of billions of neuron synapses is critically important to physical and mental health. Your senses, movements, and all bodily functions are under its control. It is what keeps you alive and makes you who you are. And it is also not a static "thing," but is actually always changing and re-structuring its connections and function based on external stimuli. Including drug use.

So to separate the physical from the mental addiction is a pretty ridiculous way to look at it. The cravings and altered state that marijuana use produces in the brain are every bit as physical as well as mental.

I wasn't doing anything for a while. Then I started to go back to my group once a week. I'm going to some AA meetings too, but they're all probation ordered from my arrest. Once that's clear my parents and I are going to continue going once a week.

A new way of thinking

Now, I don't try to rebel as much. I had a really rebellious attitude before. I would just tell my parents no and do what I wanted. If anything was put down in rules, I wasn't going to follow it. I thought it made me happier, but now that I'm just doing what I'm supposed to and getting stuff done, I can be myself and not be mad all the time.

Now I've learned to relate to people honestly. I used to lie like ten times a day. I was always getting caught in lies, but now I don't have to worry about that anymore.

My parents and I almost never get into fights anymore. If we do, it's over who's going to take the dog for a walk or little things like that. I used to give my mom a lot of s*** back in the day, so I try to be nice now. She really deserves it. It's kind of calm around the house now.

I lost all my old friends I used with, but I don't really want to hang out with them. I have some old friends who love computer games and are just like me. They just never got into drugs, so I can still hang out with them. And I have a bunch of new friends from my new school.

Most of my old using friends…I noticed after awhile it was me just going to hang out with them and we'd get bored. I questioned why I'd hang out with them, but I would smoke before I'd go, so it didn't really matter.

When I sobered up though, I figured out there was no point in hanging out with them. We just did nothing. Just sat around. I have a lot more friends now that do actual, functional stuff now, that I enjoy and can tune in with them.

I'd say I've really changed my attitude. If I hadn't, I'd be out with my friends right now getting high.

Looking ahead now

At the private school I'm going to they do four semesters in the time it takes to do two at a public school. I can graduate in six months [at 17 years old]. From there, there's a recording arts college where I can get a bachelors in sound tech in two years, learning about the music business. I've been taking classes like that in high school and I want to step into that. There are two large studios and two teachers who teach recording arts and music theory so they have all the high end equipment for us to use.

There are lots of theaters and other places that need people like that, but not many people are trying for those kinds of jobs. I think I can make some really good money doing that.

Lessons for parents

For parents, keep an eye on where your kids are going. If they are always leaving the house with weird excuses for why they're leaving the house, like "I'm taking the dog for a walk" or walking to a friend's house, something's going on. Or if they leave the house and come back in five minutes, or you can't find them for five minutes, those are weird things that kind of seem out of place and probably are out of place.

All the raver's candy bracelets have sayings written on them like "Disco Biscuit." Phrases that you can Google and find out what they mean. PLUR is the raver code. Peace Love Unity Respect is what it stands for. If they have gloves, that's another big one. LED strobe glasses. LED binkies [pacifiers]. LED anything. Black lights. If it seems out of place, ask them what it is and where they got it.

There's a web site to look for called Pill Reports that kids who are into ecstasy are always on. They have user reports on different types of pills. Users tell about how they used it, what's in it, what happened, if it's bad or not. It's basically an online catalog of every ecstasy pill made.

The progression I saw is that a certain segment of weed users would move on to MDMA and ecstasy. They would use it for a while, but then they wanted to stop because they got really burnt off it. They would go back to weed for a while, but then they would ramp up again to cocaine or Oxy and heroin.

You can get weed anywhere. I'd drive down to the local strip mall. That was a huge source of it. That's where I got it. The skate park was a big spot to get it too. The people who sold it ranged from 15 year-olds all the way up to 30-somethings – sometimes even parents.

There are drugs at my new private school too. There are drugs everywhere. You can't really avoid them. The first time I saw drugs was in 6th grade. It was pot and it was at school. There are always going to be a certain percentage of kids into drugs no matter what school you go to.

I've seen lots of people get out of the program and their parents are just over it by then. Because their parents just don't keep after them, those kids eventually go right back into doing the same stuff. Those kids are still sitting at home doing nothing. You need to keep on them.

Appendices

Appendix A - Glossary of Drug and Recovery Program Terms

For drug names and slang, see **Chapter 6 - Drug Information**. For an updated, online glossary, teens.drugabuse.gov/utilities/glossary.php

12 steps: The steps to recovery (and self discovery) that are the backbone of Alcoholics Anonymous. Also applies to Cocaine Anonymous, Marijuana Anonymous, Narcotics Anonymous, and Overeaters Anonymous.

3 C's: A basic tenant of Al-Anon, which says of addition; You didn't Cause it, you can't Control it, and you can't Cure it.

AA: Alcoholics Anonymous

Alcoholic: Someone who is addicted to alcohol or drugs. Most recovering drug addicts refer to themselves as alcoholics, go to AA meetings, and use the AA 12-step program for recovery.

Alcopops: Pre-mixed, sweetened alcoholic beverages that resemble soda pop, such as flavored hard liquor blends and hard lemonades.

Addiction: Dictionary definition is a "compulsive need for and use of a habit-forming substance", including tolerance and physiological symptoms upon withdrawal.

Bag: Slang for the small quantity of drugs that is typically purchased from a dealer. Also sack.

Bong: Water pipe used for smoking marijuana.

Character defects: Personality traits that addicts must address and deal with emotionally before they can move from being just clean, to being truly in recovery.

Clean: Derived from a clean drug test, meaning that the addict is no longer actively using.

Co-occuring disorders or Comorbidity: Presence of one or more psychiatric disorders along with substance abuse.

Detachment: The process of   stopping enabling behavior and

189

letting the alcoholic deal with the consequences of their actions. Don't confuse this with not loving your child. You can detach and still ensure that your teen knows you are still there with love and support when they make the right choices.

Dry Drunk: Someone who has given up drinking and using drugs, but has not made any internal or emotional changes.

Enabling: Behavior by a parent, spouse, partner, friend, or others that enables the addict to continue their bad behavior. Examples include providing material things such as money, trust, privileges, legal help, and housing, and also intangible things such as too much emotional involvement in the addict/alcoholic's life when they don't deserve it.

Hookah: Water pipe used for smoking a variety of flavored tobaccos. Typically not used for illegal drug use, but can be used for masking the smell or other activity involving drugs.

Huffing: Sniffing gas, fumes, or aerosols to get high.

Intensive Outpatient Program (IOP): Treatment program that is conducted in group meetings several days a week. Usually a first step in treatment as abuse intensifies, used as a way to educate and get the person to stop using before resorting to in-patient, residential treatment.

Kickbacks: A euphemism for party. Intended to sound more low key than a party so parents will be more inclined to let teens attend.

Normies: People who are not addicts or alcoholics.

Party Bus: Large limousines or shuttle-type buses that are rented as an alternative to a stationary party. Typically the operators of the party bus companies will "stretch" the rules to allow alcohol and even drugs on the buses to maintain business. Parents should **not** give in to pressure to rent these as transportation to proms or other legitimate parties.

Pharm Party: Parties where attendees collect prescription drugs from home medicine chests and then mix them in a container, whereupon the attendees randomly pull pills out of the container to sample.

Problem Behaviors: Deviations from normal development.

Process: The way in which a particular positive outcome is envisioned and facilitated.

Program: Usually refers to 12-step programs like AA, but can apply to any recovery program of proactive activity to stay clean and change long-term behaviors.

Raves: High energy, all-night dances that are usually advertised as safe and "drug and alcohol free" parties that are carefully supervised, but are actually dangerously over-crowded parties where your child can be exposed to rampant drug use and a high-crime environment. Ecstasy is the most frequent drug of abuse at raves.

Recovery: Working a program to stop using drugs and alcohol, and to heal and grow emotionally for long-term health and sobriety.

Relapse: Technically starting to use again after a period of sobriety. However, relapse usually starts before the alcoholic starts using again, when the old behavior returns, such as lack of integrity, not attending to responsibilities, skipping school or work, hanging out with the wrong people, and all the other behaviors that usually accompany using.

Residential: Live-in, full-time recovery facilities.

Risk and Protective Factors: Aspects of a teen's life that make drug use either more likely (risk) or more unlikely (protective), including family, school, job, peers and other relationships.

Shooting up: Using a hypodermic needle or syringe to inject drugs.

Sponsor: Someone with substantial time in AA, who then mentors others coming into the program. All people in AA are asked to find a sponsor who they work with on the 12 Steps, and who they can call in moments of temptation or trouble during their recovery.

Substance abuse: Recurring use of drugs or alcohol that is affecting the ability of the person to fulfill normal obligations.

Substance dependence: A maladaptive pattern of substance use, leading to clinically significant impairment or distress, including more long term effects such as tolerance, withdrawal, and using increasing quantities despite physical and psychological problems.

THC: The intoxicating chemical in marijuana.

Using: Taking and/or abusing drugs or alcohol.

White Knuckling: When the alcoholic tries to stop using and drinking on their own, with either a very weak program, or none at all. Typically not effective.

Appendix B - Contract for Behavior

The following is an example of a behavior contract. It is a good tool for a number of reasons:

- Details your expectations in black and white
- Takes negotiating and arguing with your teen out of the equation
- Your teen will not have any excuse for not knowing what he or she is getting into

However, remember that by the time you are implementing such a contract, you will almost always be dealing with someone who is dishonest and noncompliant. Most likely they will break the contract, but it still serves a purpose in setting up defined boundaries, which have probably eroded over the years, and making it very clear what your teen's choices are. If they choose not to follow, then you will know their mental and physical state, and that it is time to move on to the next step.

Some of the language may seem harsh, but if you reach this point, you'll understand why. It's time for your teen to make radical shifts in their lifestyle that will only take hold with radical shifts in behavior.

What do you need or want from us? Why do you want to come back?

What do you think will be different from the way things were when you left?

Nothing has really changed here in terms of our expectations if you want to live at home, and for us to support your education.

Our terms for you living at home follow. We reserve the right to make changes or add to them at our discretion.

We expect you to start living drug free.

We expect you to see a professional drug counselor for an evaluation, then follow a treatment plan completely.

You will be tested frequently for drugs.

If a drug test shows any use, you will leave our home with no possibility of returning.

We expect you to be courteous and respectful to everyone in the family. This includes verbal respect as well as respectful behavior. We will be courteous towards you. Please do not confuse this with having an "equal say" about how things are done. You don't have an equal say.

We expect you to participate and assist in the cleaning and maintenance of our home, including the care of pets. We all need to work together.

We expect you to comply with the rules and standards of our home, even if you don't agree. When you have your own place and pay your own bills, then you can make the rules and set your own standards. The following rules apply:

- TV – Several channels will be blocked from access. We will also not record episodes of [insert limited programs here] and similar programs. We will not watch porn, soft porn, or anything either of us feel condones drug use, or is offensive or degrading in nature. Some channels offering these programs may not be blocked, but you still need to comply with our guidelines. Video games will be limited to [X] days a week, for [X] hours per day.

- Going out – Initially you will not be allowed to socialize outside our home. This is a privilege that will be earned through your success in the drug program and with a positive attitude.

- Friends – With your success in a drug program and a positive attitude you can earn visiting with friends. Plan on friends coming over here more than they have in the past. Your old friends may not be receptive to this, however, we hope you will make new friends who encourage you through your recovery.

- Alcohol use – You are underage and should not be drinking alcohol. You will be tested for alcohol consumption. If we find that you have been drinking, you will lose all privileges and you will return to living in the [garage/tent]. You will start over towards earning privileges as well as our trust.

- Cigarettes – We do not smoke in our house or on our property. If we find cigarettes, lighters or any type of smoking paraphernalia in our home or on our property, it will be destroyed.

You will need to get a part-time job. We will no longer pay for your entertainment. You will earn your own spending money.

You will not damage our home in any way. You will be expected to stay out of rooms that are locked and out of areas you are told to stay away from. If you damage our home or enter "our space," you will be locked out of the home and will be able to enter only when we are home. Any repairs will be paid for out of your savings account.

You will respect our resources in terms of water use and the use of our appliances. You will lose the privileges of showering and washing your clothes here if you will not follow these and other simple requests. We pay the bills and we all need to conserve where we can and take care of our belongings.

Privileges that you can earn back:

- Time with friends outside our home
- Paying for college
- We will pay for community college for the first year. Based on your performance, we will pay for your education at a four-year university.
- Continued support through your program and your life
- Family vacations, short trips, baseball games
- Driving our car
- [List other positive things your teen can earn back to incentivize them to change].

IMPORTANT: We are united with this. You will no longer play us against one another. We both work very hard and we have a right to live in a happy, clean, peaceful environment and one we can look forward to coming home to at the end of the day.

Appendix C - Links and Resources

Note: The links and resources in this book are provided as information only. This information does not constitute an endorsement and/or guarantee of the veracity or effectiveness of any service or program listed here by the authors or W. Wooton Inc.

Addiction Treatment Search

www.addictionsearch.com

Drug abuse statistics, directories, and counseling resources.

Addiction Journal

www.addictionjournal.net

A compilation of thoughts, skills, and emotion to help other parents struggling with an addicted child.

Boarding Schools Directory

www.boardingschoolsinfo.com

Lots of information on boarding schools, how to choose one, and school listings.

Drug Information for Teens

www.teens.drugabuse.gov

Sister site to NIDA, written for teens.

Drug Rehab.com

www.drug-rehab.com

"Connecting people with people who can help". Includes lots of information and listings of rehab facilities, mostly in California.

FreeFromHell.com

www.freefromhell.com

Social help network for addicts, families, and friends.

GetSmart About Drugs
www.getsmartaboutdrugs.com

Just Think Twice – You've heard the fiction. Now learn the facts.
www.justthinktwice.com

NAADAC: Association for Addiction Professionals
www.naadac.org

National Institute on Drug Abuse
www.NIDA.org
National information organization and database on drugs and their abuse.

Monitoring the Future
www.monitoringthefuture.org
Ongoing survey and study of behaviors, attitudes, and values of American secondary school students, college students, and young adults by the NIDA and the University of Michigan.

Office of National Drug Control Policy
www.whitehousedrugpolicy.gov/drugfact
Very comprehensive listing of facts and information on drugs, including street terms.

Oxy Watchdog
www.oxywatchdog.com
Current news and trends about Oxy abuse.

Pacific Treatment Services
www.PacificTreatmentServices.com
Substance abuse and behavioral counseling for teens in the San Diego area run by Will Wooton, CADC.

Parent to Parent

addictionprofiler.blogspot.com

One parent tells about her experience and others respond.

Smart Recovery

www.smartrecovery.org

"Scientific", self-empowering addiction recovery support group.

SOBERINFO

www.soberinfo.com

Linking the global sobriety community.

Spector Pro

www.spectorsoft.com

Record and monitor your teen's computer activity on PCs or MACs.

Substance Abuse and Mental Health Services Administration

www.samhsa.gov

Reducing the impact of substance abuse and mental illness on America's communities through 8 Strategic Initiatives that focus on improving lives and capitalizing on emerging opportunities.

Troubled Teen Blog

www.troubledteenblog.com

Support for families with troubled teens.

Yahoo Directory

dir.yahoo.com

Search Residential Programs for Children (no quotes) for a directory of facilities, and links to other directories and resources.

12-step Programs:

Alcoholics Anonymous
www.aa.org

Al-Anon support group for families and siblings
www.al-anon.alateen.org

Cocaine Anonymous
www.ca.org

Marijuana Anonymous
www.marijuana-anonymous.org

Narcotics Anonymous
www.na.org

Nar-Anon
www.nar-anon.org

Nicotine Anonymous
www.nicotine-anonymous.org

Overeaters Anonymous
www.oa.org

The Authors

Will Wooton, LAADC, CADC

William Wooton, an LAADC, CAADAC certified alcohol and drug addiction counselor, has been working in addiction treatment helping adolescents and families for over 15 years. His passion for working with addicted teens started when he became sober himself at the age of 16. After experiencing firsthand what recovery can do, he decided that helping others and their families was his career path.

During his career as a counselor he has facilitated thousands of groups on addiction behaviors. Each week, he conducts several, weekly, open-to-the-public education and support groups that have continued for over a decade.

After starting in private practice in 1997 he founded Pacific Treatment Services (PTS) in 2005. As director of PTS, his focus is on building effective outpatient programs and developing new support services for teens and their families.

Bruce Rowe, writer

Bruce Rowe is a former business reporter who has been a corporate marketing writer and public relations professional for more than 25 years. At the *San Diego Business Journal* he developed a reputation as a top newsroom producer and was known for quickly and accurately capturing and communicating the essence of the companies he covered. Mr. Rowe's writing experience includes feature articles, white papers, case studies, marketing brochures, press releases, web content, broadcast copy, video scripts, and short stories.

As a father, Mr. Rowe has lived the process described in this book, watching his own son follow the path of experimentation, increased use, addiction, and recovery. He has firsthand knowledge of the parental denial and rationalization that enable a child to continue their use into the dangerous territory of drug abuse and addiction. Through the techniques in this book, and the grace of God, his son now lives a sober, productive life of recovery.

Connect with us for more information online:

Pacific Treatment Services: www.PacificTreatmentServices.com
Blog: www.PacificTreatmentServices.com/blog
Facebook: www.facebook.com/PacificTreatmentServices